A Catholic Perspective

on

The Purpose Driven Life

A Catholic Perspective on
The Purpose Driven Life

Father Joseph M. Champlin

CATHOLIC BOOK PUBLISHING CORP.
New Jersey

IMPRIMATUR: ✚ Most Reverend Thomas J. Costello, D.D.

Vicar General, Diocese of Syracuse, New York
Solemnity of Saints Peter and Paul
June 29, 2006

First published in September, 2006 by

Catholic Book Publishing Corp.

77 West End Road

Totowa, NJ 07512

Copyright © 2006 by Joseph M. Champlin

ISBN 0-89942-132-6

Library of Congress Catalog Card Number: 2006930090

Cover design by Beth DeNapoli

Printed in the United States of America

1 2 3 4 5 6 7 8 9

www.catholicbookpublishing.com

Contents

Acknowledgments

THIS somewhat unique publication became a reality only because of the assistance of these people to whom I am deeply indebted:

- ➤ The two small groups whose six-week sessions on "Developing A Purpose Driven and Stress-Free Life" led to my reflections which are the heart of this text.
- ➤ Michael Leach, veteran editor, publisher of Orbis Books, and a longtime friend, who gave me wise advice when the book was only an idea.
- ➤ Robert Cavalero of Catholic Book Publishing Corporation and Emilie Cerar of Resurrection Press who saw the concept's value and worked very hard to bring it to completion.
- ➤ Patricia Livingston, author, lecturer and friend, whose constructive suggestion nipped a major problem in the beginning stages and made the eventual content much more coherent.
- ➤ Doug Lockhart and the people at Zondervan Corporation, publisher of *The Purpose Driven Life*, together with Pastor Rick Warren of Saddleback Church whose incredibly successful hardcover book prompted this Roman Catholic perspective on his message.
- ➤ Bishop Thomas J. Costello, whose editorial skills and current position have made this a better text while also giving it official Roman Catholic Church approval.
- ➤ Ann Tyndall, who again has transformed difficult to decipher hand-written pages into a computerized, easy to follow manuscript.

Introduction

RICK Warren, the energetic founder and shepherd of Saddleback Church in Southern California, is perhaps the currently best-known clergyperson in the United States.

His hard-cover book, *The Purpose Driven Life* has sold in excess of 25 million copies and has been on the *New York Times* best seller list for 130 weeks. Both *The New Yorker* and *Fortune* magazines have published lengthy feature articles about him. *Time* described—with photos—his journey to Rwanda and his vision of a 5-7 year self-sufficiency project for that African country, site of the genocide in 1994. An Atlanta woman drew immediate national attention to his book when she used its message successfully to persuade a violent fugitive holding her hostage to surrender to the police.

On a more personal level, a relative of mine and her husband, both Episcopalians, use the book as an ongoing source of inspiration. In addition, a Catholic friend has found *The Purpose Driven Life* helpful in connecting spiritually with her Jewish husband.

As a Roman Catholic priest for over 50 years, I regularly check to see what are the currently favorite films and books as possible resources for preaching, teaching and writing. That interest led me to Warren's book.

After reading the text, I organized for a local retreat house "Developing A Purpose Driven and Stress Free Life: A Six Week, Forty Day Program" based on Warren's book and *Slow Down* a small paperback of my own. Forty people signed up for the sessions and thirty persevered until the end.

Six months later at a different retreat house I repeated the experience. A remarkably large number—103—signed up for the sessions with most of them in attendance each night.

Each weekly 90-minute session involved an extended period of biblical reflective prayer, group sharing, a brief presentation about stress, plus a lengthy presentation of a Catholic perspective on one section of Warren's book.

The present book grew out of these events. Those Catholic perspective reflections have been expanded and connected more precisely to *The Purpose Driven Life*.

My text has been directed to Roman Catholics. However, I hope that persons with interest in comparative religious studies or in current spirituality approaches, especially from a Christian perspective, will find the material informative and inspirational.

Catholics, having read *The Purpose Driven Life*, probably discovered that, in general, Pastor Warren's words proved very helpful for their spiritual journeys. At the same time, they may have met a few bumps in the road, occasional statements or suggestions that raised questions in their minds or made them feel somewhat uncomfortable.

Their inquiries could perhaps be summarized in this fashion: Is that particular point a Roman Catholic way of thinking, believing or acting? Does the official Church have something to say about this subject?

My book seeks to accomplish two goals: to clarify those issues under question and to enrich Warren's teachings with a Catholic input.

A good example of such *clarification* occurs in my first chapter.

On Day Four, "Made to Last Forever," Pastor Warren states that "In heaven we will be reunited with loved ones who are believers" (p. 39). Incidentally, citations are from the hardcover edition of *The Purpose Driven Life*. My *clarification* mentions that "I would read into this prediction an acceptance of what evangelical preachers in general seemingly believe and teach: only those who explicitly accept Jesus as Savior will receive the reward of heaven." The clarification then cites current official Roman Catholic teaching which follows a different path.

An illustration of *enrichment* centers around the sacred forty days concept. In his introduction, "A Journey with Purpose," Rick Warren cites eight biblical examples showing that God considers 40 days a spiritually significant time period. Whenever God wanted to prepare someone for a divinely determined purpose, the Creator took 40 days to do so. The practical application of this is that readers giving 40 days to *The Purpose Driven Life* will likewise prepare and transform their own lives.

The enrichment section in chapter one of my book, under "The sacred forty days," describes in detail how that forty day notion dominates the Roman Catholic observance of Lent.

For the most effective use of this study guide, I would suggest following Pastor Warren's day- to-day approach for a particular section, then, after completing that portion, read the corresponding chapter in my book.

For example, read Warren's "A Journey with Purpose," (pp. 9-13) and follow for seven days the section "What On Earth Am I Here For?" (pp. 17-53). After reading and reflecting on that material, turn to the first chapter of *this* book, "My Purpose on Earth."

Repeat this process for the forty days of Rick Warren's volume.

As I witnessed in those six-week events described above, doing this as a group experience enhances the process and can be very effective.

While reading *The Purpose Driven Life*, Catholics who encounter one of those bumps in the road might make a note of what the question is and where it arose. They could then either immediately check the clarification portion in my book to see if the issue is dealt with there or wait until the seven days have been completed, revisit the noted bumps and seek the clarification at that time.

People today may be less religious, that is fewer attend church regularly or become members of specific congregations, but there is no doubt that an increasing hunger for spirituality exists. More and more persons are concerned about prayer and the spiritual life, about God and eternity, about the search for inner happiness and the ultimate purpose of life here on earth.

The incredible success of Pastor Rick Warren's book is clear proof of that. So, too, the popularity of my own sixty second radio spots, "Spiritual Suggestions to De-Stress Your Day," with the concluding tag line, "You may have tried everything else, why not try God," underscores that hunger.

Moreover, in terms of numbers and enthusiasm the two sessions I organized about "Developing A Purpose Driven and Stress-free Life" demonstrate deep desires for prayer, meditation or reflection, and an interior life.

For many years during the first half of the last century, and even earlier than that, most Catholics memorized a catechism answer to this question: "Why did God make you?" The response: "God made me to know, love and serve God in this world, and be happy with God in the next life."

Our purpose: to follow in Jesus' footsteps here on earth and live with Christ forever in heaven.

Pastor Rick Warren believes that following his book for 40 days will impact and transform a person's life. I hope and pray that my companion study guide will likewise assist others, especially Roman Catholics, in such a transformation process.

Father Joseph M. Champlin
Our Lady of Good Counsel
Warners, New York
Lent, 2006

Chapter 1

My Purpose on Earth

(Warren's "A Journey with Purpose" Pages 9-12
"What on Earth Am I Here For?"—Days 1-7)

Roman Catholic teaching and practice coincide with some parts of Pastor Rick Warren's message in his book *The Purpose Driven Life* and clash with other points. There is, however, more agreement than disagreement.

This and subsequent chapters will give a Catholic perspective on Rick Warren's publication. It will affirm and enrich parts where the two seemingly coincide. It will explain and clarify points where the two apparently clash.

Differences and Clarifications

❖ Providence and Freedom

In his book, Pastor Warren stresses that God has a precise plan for each one of us. The Creator has "prescribed every single detail of your body." God has, he teaches, planned our birth, our death, the place where we are born and where we will live. Warren maintains that all elements of our lives are part of God's plan and purpose for us. However, he does acknowledge that the Creator takes into account human error and sin (Day 2).

Roman Catholics, on the other hand, struggle to balance their belief in God's loving providence and in the

Creator's gift of human freedom. We embrace that challenge as a mystery, as an aspect of the divine never fully to be grasped in this life.

How can a transcendent God be with us at every moment, guide us and protect us, yet step back, cherish and respect our freedom to make the many choices we face in life?

This mysterious blend of providence and freedom becomes most confusing at times of tragedy—when a young child accidentally falls from a five-story building and dies, when a person is fatally injured by a drunk driver, when terrorists crash two planes into New York City's Twin Towers.

The 9/11 attack brought this dilemma into sharp focus for Americans. Some people cried out, "How could God do this? Why did God let this happen?" Parents of that deceased child and the family of the person killed in the auto accident, as well as others stunned by similar dark events, may ask identical questions.

The response that this was part of God's plan or that a good God has called the person home hardly comforts those who are grieving and seems theologically inaccurate.

A better reply might imagine God saying:

"The 9/11 disaster was not part of my plan. I could have prevented this tragedy, but in doing so I would have deprived human beings of freedom, of their ability to love or hate, to choose the good or the bad. But once those choices are made and the event happens, I bring good out of the bad, light out of darkness. And I am close to the brokenhearted, those who are crushed in spirit, giving them strength, courage and comfort."

✤ Who will be saved?

Perhaps the sharpest difference between what Pastor Warren proclaims in his book and what the Catholic Church teaches concerns the question of salvation. Who will be saved? What people get to heaven?

He promises that "In heaven we will be reunited with loved ones who are believers." As I indicated in the Introduction, I would read into this prediction an acceptance of what evangelical preachers in general seemingly believe and teach: only those who explicitly accept Jesus as Savior will receive the reward of heaven (Day 4).

Current official Roman Catholic teaching follows a different path.

Around a half century ago, Father Leonard Feeney, a New England priest, maintained that only those who are actually members of the Roman Catholic Church will be saved and enter heaven. The Latin phrase, *"Extra ecclesiam nulla salus,"* "outside the Church, there is no salvation," summarizes his position. He strongly advocated that notion, preached it and gained a significant following. Eventually, Vatican authorities rejected his views and ordered him both to retract this teaching and to cease preaching it.

The most contemporary compendium of official Catholic teaching is the *Catechism of the Catholic Church*. A single paragraph, echoing the teaching of the Second Vatican Council forty years before publication of the *Catechism*, summarizes the Church's present position on "Who will be saved?" While not denying the importance and value of accepting the Church and Jesus as Lord, it holds that the door to heaven is open for all those who faithfully follow the lights with which God has illuminated their hearts.

Since Christ died for all, and since all men are in fact called to one and the same destiny, which is divine, we must hold that the Holy Spirit offers to all the possibility of being made partakers, in a way known to God, of the Paschal mystery. Every man who is ignorant of the Gospel of Christ and of his Church, but seeks the truth and does the will of God in accordance with his understanding of it, can be saved. It may be supposed that such persons would have *desired Baptism explicitly* if they had known its necessity (Article 1260).

> *. . . the door to heaven is open for all those who faithfully follow the lights with which God has illuminated their hearts.*

Affirmation and Enrichment

✤ The sacred forty days

Pastor Warren cites frequent instances in the Bible during which individuals or groups of people were transformed in preparation for a unique sacred event in "A Journey with Purpose."

As the Saddleback pastor observes, forty days have special significance in the Bible. Noah spent 40 days in the ark and Moses 40 on Mount Sinai; God gave the city of Nineveh 40 days to change; Jesus prepared for his public ministry by 40 days of prayer and fasting in the desert and, after his resurrection, continued to transform his disciples for 40 days until he returned to his Father in heaven.

Lent for Roman Catholics has that same dimension. We arrive at the forty day figure by beginning with Ash Wednesday, counting the days to Easter, and then subtracting the Sundays. The Lord's Day is meant for joyful celebration of the Resurrection rather than for penitential purification of the soul. In fact, some spiritual leaders suggest that we discontinue our Lenten sacrifices on Sundays and resume them on Mondays. In that way, we remind ourselves each week of Jesus' victory over sin and death and then, with a fresh start, begin a new week of penitential practices.

The overall purpose of Lenten prayer, fasting and works of charity is twofold: first, to prepare for the initial reception of baptism (adults seeking to enter the church) or a renewal of baptismal promises (those already members of the church); secondly, to enter more deeply into the passion of Christ. The initial part of Lent focuses on the baptism aspect; the latter portion of this season centers on the Lord's suffering.

✤ Mega or full-service churches

Charles Truehart, an Episcopalian journalist, spent a year studying several of the mega or full-service churches in the United States. In his August 1996 essay for *Atlantic Monthly*, he described certain elements common to all of them: ample parking, attractive landscaping, clear signage, clean bathrooms, warm hospitality, singable songs, practical preaching and a multiplicity of self-help groups dealing with the real issues of members such as various addictions or marriage challenges.

The Saddleback Church certainly includes those ingredients, but Pastor Warren began and developed his large (22,000 members) faith community through small groups which met each week for prayer, bible sharing and discussion.

An impressive dimension of the Saddleback Church and of Rick Warren's vision is a concern for those in need here and abroad. Significant donations of money and personnel have been given to help, for example, victims of Katrina in the United States and of poverty in Africa.

Some visionary Roman Catholic parishes have sought to implement several of these successful pastoral approaches, although many are limited in doing so for various practical reasons. New, large, suburban churches are better able to introduce some of those elements common to megachurches. In addition, the shortage of priests has led to consolidation of parishes which may ultimately lead to constructing one large church to care for several smaller units. Those planners look to the pattern of full-service churches with the hope that it will work for Roman Catholics. It remains to be seen if those attempts succeed.

In general, Roman Catholic leaders ponder with wonder, but also with questions, the remarkable growth and vitality of megachurches like Saddleback, conscious that some of its members were formerly Catholic.

✤ Multiple translations

Rick Warren cites approximately 15 different translations of biblical texts throughout his book. Modern scholars now translate the Bible from the original languages. A number of such versions are acceptable to and used by Roman Catholics. The most common is *The New American Bible* "translated from the original languages with critical use of all the ancient sources," and approved by the United States bishops.

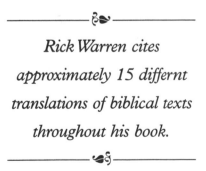

Rick Warren cites approximately 15 differnt translations of biblical texts throughout his book.

However, Roman Catholic public worship, particularly the Eucharistic Liturgy or Mass, follows a special translation of readings published in a Lectionary approved by the American bishops and by Vatican authorities. While Roman Catholics are free to use other translations for private reading and study, week after week, over a three-year cycle, they hear the Lectionary version of the Scripture excerpts.

During the past decade there have been rather strong controversies within the Catholic Church over the translation of the official Lectionary. The debates have centered around the use of more inclusive language on the one hand, and the relative merits of a literal, rather than a more contemporary translation of the original Latin text on the other.

❖ Products not prisoners of the past

Warren's emphasis that "God specializes in giving people a fresh start" perfectly coincides with Catholic teachings on the compassion of Jesus as Savior and God's promise to care for our needs in the future (Day 3). Spiritual leaders often offer this practical advice to individuals: "Leave the past to God's mercy, the future to God's providence, and live fully the present moment."

Guilt

As Warren states so well, we are products, but need not be prisoners of the past.

For over three decades I have conducted an annual retreat or mission in parishes across this country. They begin with a homily at all the weekend Masses and follow with three evening sessions. The Saturday evening and Sunday morning message centers on "No Pain, No Gain: Sin and Guilt, Forgiveness and Peace." After establishing the necessity and nature of a healthy sense of sin through numerous examples, I describe true and false guilt, illustrating the deep pain it causes together with the consequent need for divine forgiveness and healing. The homily then seeks to create a warm image of Jesus as Savior, who in word and deed frequently showed God's mercy which can both forgive our guilt and heal our hearts. It also casts the Catholic sacrament of penance, reconciliation or confession in an appealing light.

The message is for all present, but it has a particular impact on the few who are carrying a heavy burden of sin and guilt, sometimes for many years. The positive reaction to this presentation has always been most encouraging.

This letter is a rather dramatic illustration of the responses.

I felt so compelled to write a short note, and tell you of the changes that are taking place in my life. You may not remember me, but a few weeks ago your intercession with the Lord changed my life. I had carried my guilt for over fifty years and the mission gave me the strength and courage to receive the Sacrament of Reconciliation. I had prayed to be able to do this for so very, very long—to remove the pain and guilt I felt—and God led me to you and the mission. My life has changed. I feel at peace and close to the Lord. God bless you and the good work you do in his name. You are forever in my prayers.

Resentment

All of us have been hurt or wounded in the past by someone's word, deed or omission. That can generate resentment or, even worse, hatred. Until we let go of those inner feelings or attitudes, a deep peace will not be ours. Moreover, in Warren's words, we can thus be driven by this resentment or anger.

Unfortunately, our minds tend to keep replaying, like a tape, the hurtful event or experience, which in turn resuscitates inner feelings. Concentrating on the now moment and consciously turning our mind away from the past can swiftly dissipate the negativity and enable us to move forward with serenity and purpose.

Detachment

At a session with over 100 persons discussing *The Purpose Driven Life*, several indicated that its teaching about less attachment to the here and now with more focus on the eternity to come made an immediate impact upon their lives. One, in particular, found helpful James Dobson's story about his tennis trophy— once proudly displayed in the school's trophy cabinet, but, years later, during a building renovation, simply removed and thrown into a trash can (p. 33).

❖ Focus on forever

In parallel fashion the Saddleback pastor's stress on the human hunger for immortality and God's plan for our eternal future closely parallels Roman Catholic teaching and practice (Day 4). "You have an inborn instinct that longs for immortality," Warren proclaims, contrasting our relatively brief time on earth with the prospect that we will "spend forever in eternity."

Priest, educator and columnist for the *New York Times*, Monsignor Lorenzo Albacete, in his book *God at the Ritz: Attraction to Infinity*, frequently remarks that the human heart longs for the timeless, the eternal, the immortal. Moreover, Roman Catholic rituals from baptism to funerals and constantly in between, repeatedly mention that

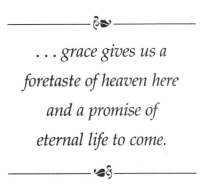

. . . grace gives us a foretaste of heaven here and a promise of eternal life to come.

grace gives us a foretaste of heaven here and a promise of eternal life to come.

This chapter on the first section of *The Purpose Driven Life* should indicate that Roman Catholics are in total agreement with many of Pastor Rick Warren's teachings. However, it will also surface the need, or at least the helpfulness, of a Catholic perspective on some points in his book.

Chapter 2

Friendship with God

(Warren's Purpose #1:
"You Were Planned for God's Pleasure" Days 8-14)

A S in the first chapter, we offer some clarifications where there are differences between Rick Warren's teaching in *The Purpose Driven Life* and a Catholic perspective on the same issues. Next, where there is agreement, I offer affirmation and enrichment of those points based on Roman Catholic doctrines and practices.

Differences and Clarifications

❖ An Unchanging God

Pastor Rick Warren stresses the unchanging nature of God, a good and loving, all-powerful God who notices every detail of our lives, is in control, has a plan for our lives, and will save us (Day 14).

Those truths became real to me one dark evening at a Benedictine monastery in New York State. After an especially difficult and trying event in my life, I traveled there to visit with the wise and learned abbot with whom I had been acquainted. After listening to my serious troubles, he simply remarked, "God's love for us is constant." No lengthy words of advice or comforting observations. Merely a soft but strong statement about the Creator's unchanging love for us.

However, a mystery to be experienced enters the discussion. At this point we reflect upon Jesus, the Son of Mary, who wept on occasion, felt annoyed at other times and knew sadness in the Garden of Olives. However, as Son of God, he also walked on water, healed the sick and raised the dead. We never completely comprehend that mystery of Christ, fully human and fully divine.

We pray not to change our unchangeable God, but to change ourselves or let ourselves be changed.

There is a practical conclusion here. We pray not to change our unchangeable God, but to change ourselves or let ourselves be changed.

✤ Mary

Just as Christian, Jewish and Muslim adherents commonly share belief in weekly community worship and daily personal prayer, so there seems an initial, but growing convergence around Mary, the mother of Jesus.

That recognition of her might not be articulated by Semitic leaders, but the fact that Mary was a Jewish maiden, and presumably very orthodox in her religious practice, establishes a basis for mutual discussions about this possible commonality.

Jaroslav Pelikan, history professor at Yale University, notes in his book, *Mary Through the Centuries*, that Mary is the most often pronounced female name in the western world. Moreover, he states that she has been portrayed in art and music more than any other woman in history.

Among Muslims, Mary ("Maryan") is the only woman's name mentioned in the Qur'ăn or the Koran. In addition, sūrah number 19, one of the longest chapters in the Koran, describes in some detail the angels' annunciation to Mary. It resembles the account in Luke's gospel 1:26-38.

Mary ("Maryan") is the only woman's name mentioned in the Qur'a˘n or the Koran.

The angelic visitors said "God has chosen you and made you pure and exalted above womankind . . . His name is Messiah, Jesus son of Mary."

Currently there has been a major shift among Christians with regard to Mary.

Roman Catholics have always given great honor to Mary as the Mother of Jesus, the Son of God. While acknowledging that she is only human, not divine, they nevertheless address her with this familiar petition, "Holy Mary, Mother of God, pray for us.

Mainline Protestants continue to reject both the title "Mother of God" for Mary and the type of Catholic devotion given to her. But in recent times, more and more leaders in these denominations, have begun to make Mary part of their religious tradition. However, their approach would see her as Saint Mary, a holy woman to be imitated, not the intermediary interceding with her Son Jesus on our behalf.

Pastor Rick Warren may fall into that category. He teaches that "God chose Mary to be the Mother of Jesus, not because she was talented or wealthy or beautiful, but because she was totally surrendered to him" (Day 10).

There has been a resurrection of interest among some Roman Catholics who grew up with an intense devotion honoring Mary, abandoned it during their years of "enlightenment," but have renewed it in their later lives.

Well-known novelist, Mary Gordon, speaks about "Coming to Terms with Mary" in a *Commonweal* article (1/15/82). The author longed to do so as she became older, particularly when experiencing motherhood for the first time. Mary now models "innocence, grief, and glory" for Gordon and the novelist can relate to that image of Jesus' mother.

Sally Cunneen, editor of a theological journal and author of *In Search of Mary*, writing in the *Notre Dame Magazine* (12/81), remarked that "the lovely lady dressed in blue" image of Mary seemed far from reality in her early years and like many Catholics she tucked away her rosary.

Currently, however, Ms. Cunneen believes that those same people "have begun to see that Jesus' mother has more to do with our reality than we once thought. Now we need a new understanding of Mary which allows us to reclaim her."

Cunneen and some others have discovered in the *Magnificat* Mary as an assertive woman concerned about social justice. That prayer's phrases, "He has pulled down princes from their thrones and exalted the lowly . . . the hungry he has filled with good things, the rich sent empty away," echoed the aspirations of contemporary activists seeking structural changes to make this a better world through a just peace.

For many decades during the last century, Roman Catholics at the end of Mass added Hail Marys seeking the conversion of Russia and the end of communism. There appeared to be no answer to those prayerful pleas for years. Then suddenly the entire communistic empire seemed to collapse and this ideology lost much of its power or force.

Perhaps Mary the Mother of Jesus, honored jointly as we described by Christian and Muslim people (and in a sense by Jewish persons) may dissolve hatred and violence, thus bringing love and peace to this troubled world.

Affirmation and Enrichment

❖ Weekly Worship

Worshiping weekly is a common practice among Christian, Jewish and Muslim people. For most Christians, the Sabbath observance is on Sunday when Jesus rose from the dead; for Jewish persons, the Sabbath observance occurs from sundown Friday through sundown Saturday; for Muslim people, their weekly public worship takes place generally in a Mosque on Friday around noon.

✤ Praise and Gratitude

Christian, Jewish and Muslim believers likewise share a common ideal: giving praise and gratitude to God should form a central aspect of their religious lives.

Muslims are expected to stop five times each day and recite a prayer or *salat* on their knees facing Mecca with foreheads touching the ground. The prayerful words are directed to Allah, the Beneficent, the Merciful, the one divine, transcendent, omnipotent God. These prayerful intervals occur at dawn, afternoon, late afternoon, after sunset and at night.

Not too long ago a clerk at the gift shop in a hotel near the Toronto airport, seeing my Roman collar, proudly announced that he was a Muslim. He then immediately went to a cupboard, removed his prayer mat and mentioned that customers were very understanding when he interrupted his work to recite the designated words of praise and gratitude.

Certain devout Jewish believers seek to recite 100 times daily a *berakah* phrase which praises or blesses God for various minor or major gifts received; for example, improved health, water for washing, food at mealtime.

Christians read in the New Testament that Jesus often gave thanks to the Father. Christ also taught his followers the importance of being grateful to the Giver of all gifts through the famous story of ten cured lepers, with only one returning to express gratitude. For Christian traditions with a strong eucharistic emphasis, like Catholics and the Mass, Jesus' example at the Last Supper is pivotal in their belief and practice. As recorded in the three synoptic gospels and Paul's first letter to the Corinthians, Christ "gave thanks" before his words over the bread and wine. The very word "eucharist," taken from the Greek, means to give thanks.

✤ Surrender

Joseph Cardinal Bernardin, the late chief shepherd for the archdiocese of Chicago, wrote *Gift of Peace*, his reflections on three different experiences in the latter part of his life. They included a successful struggle with cancer; the false, but very public accusation that he had molested a young seminary student when he was stationed in Cincinnati; and a second bout with cancer which eventually ended with his death.

A central theme of his book, an attitude which emerged from those three painful events, was the need in such situations to let go, to surrender, to place one-self totally in God's care. His deep prayer life enabled him to do this and brought great peace to this distinguished church leader.

I recently visited, at the family's request, a late middle aged man in the hospital with liver failure. He had retired after several decades as an elementary public school principal. During the visit he, knowing that death was imminent, mentioned his desire or attempt to let go spiritually, "abandoning himself into God's loving hands," the same phrase Cardinal Bernardin had employed.

I asked if he would care to receive the Church's sacrament for the anointing of the sick. When this very ill man nodded affirmatively, I proceeded with the ritual of biblical readings and prayers, the silent laying on of hands, and anointing his forehead and hands with blessed oil. He died several days later.

——————— ᙭ ———————

. . . the anointing ceremony significantly aided him in the letting go, surrendering-to-God process.

——————— ᙭ ———————

During the calling hours and the funeral, over a half dozen family members remarked how this sacramental action seemed to bring great peace to their loved one. He had related to them on several occasions that our visit and the anointing ceremony significantly aided him in the letting go, surrendering-to-God process.

A deeply frightened middle-aged woman facing a carotid artery surgical procedure likewise experienced the peace-giving power of the sacrament for the sick. Two friends brought her to church and, after the priest had done so, one by one they laid their hands upon the woman's head. The priest then anointed her on the forehead and hands and also traced consecrated oil along her neck where the incision would occur.

She experienced an immediate calming of her fears and, two weeks later, reappeared in church, relating the surgeon's comment that he had never witnessed such a rapid healing of the wounded area.

❖ Faith and Feelings

We often use the term celebration in connection with sacred services. It becomes quite natural to then compare these spiritual celebration events with secular events such as birthdays, weddings, and anniversaries. These latter occasions tend to have an upbeat, joyous feeling. Applying that pattern in a univocal way to worship raises problematic issues.

Two quite different examples may clarify this point.

- On Easter Sunday, the liturgy committee of a Catholic parish wished to celebrate Christ's resurrection in a creative way. To accomplish this, they provided departing worshipers with colorful inflated balloons, each one containing a brief message of greeting to those who would eventually receive them. They all crossed the street to a parking lot and, upon the shouted signal, let them go.

  The rising balloons created a majestic image, but, unfortunately polluted the environment and probably killed some birds who ingested them.

The organizers rejoiced and acclaimed: "That was a real celebration."

- When the young spouse and mother of three, all under five, died suddenly and unexpectedly in her sleep, the grief of her husband, family, friends and community was enormous. An overflow crowd gathered in church for her funeral Mass. It, too, was a celebration of Christ's resurrection, but hardly possessed an upbeat, joyous feeling.

Personal prayer and worship services are essentially faith experiences. Our faith may overflow into our feelings, but not necessarily. A faith-filled celebration may lack a feeling component. Contrariwise, a feeling-filled celebration may lack any substantial element of faith. However, God is generous beyond our comprehension. Our faith celebrations frequently do possess a joyous, upbeat feeling content. But when that is lacking, as in the funeral example, the prayer and worship may nevertheless be rich faith events.

The critical aspect of private prayer and public worship for Christians is an encounter, a meeting with Jesus in faith.

The critical aspect of private prayer and public worship for Christians is an encounter, a meeting with Jesus in faith.

❖ Dark Night of Sense and Soul

When people embark upon a steady and serious path of prayer, they may in the beginning find the road smooth and the consolations frequent. That may be the divine way of encouraging beginners.

But often those regular prayer practitioners experience periods of dryness and darkness. The sensible consolations disappear or an impenetrable wall surfaces which apparently halts all connection with God.

Those dark nights of sense and soul obviously can prove quite disconcerting. Have I done something wrong? Am I praying in the wrong way? Has God abandoned me?

The answer to those earnest inquiries is "no." These are purification or testing periods, our faith being purified by fire, much as precious metals are cleansed by the flames and heat of a commercial furnace.

Spiritual guides like St. John of the Cross (d. 1582) and Teresa of Avila (d. 1591) categorized and described these spiritual phenomena. They labeled them as the Dark Night of the Sense and Soul or the Purgative, Illuminative and Unitive Stages.

The Marriage Encounter Movement which enjoyed enormous popularity in the 1960s and '70s followed a somewhat similar approach to married life (and the priesthood and religious life as well). Couples, priests and nuns tend to experience Romance, Disillusionment and Joy stages in their lives. These are not chronological, automatic or fixed moments, but an awareness of them can relieve a person's anxiety and turn them into occasions for growth.

John Cardinal O'Connor passed through a terribly dark spiritual time while serving as a chaplain in Okinawa. His faith in the most elemental aspects of his life—God, the Church, the priesthood, the Eucharist—suddenly vanished.

For several months he prayed at length in absolute spiritual darkness, clinging to these truths, hanging on by his fingertips.

This dry, painful, dark period finally passed and a profound peace came over him. His faith never again wavered.

Chapter 3

Members of God's Family

(Warren's Purpose #2:
"You Were Formed for God's Family" Days 15-21)

A POCKET-SIZED dictionary lists several meanings for the word "church." It could designate a building for public worship, a religious service, all Christians, a particular Christian denomination, or a religious congregation.

Purpose #2, chapters for Days 15-21, describe Pastor Warren's definition or vision of church as God's Family. Here are some of the key elements.

- Faith in Jesus is the one essential condition for membership (p. 118).

- The church is the Body of Christ, "a body, not a building; an organism, not an organization" (p. 131).

- Small groups or cells make up the Body of Christ, the church, and are like the lifeboats attached to a ship. The 400-500 small groups which make up the 20,000 plus members of his Saddleback Church are examples of that structure (p. 139).

- Frequent contact with the group (presumably both the small cell and the Sunday worshiping assembly) is expected and necessary to build genuine relationships (p. 150).

- Oneness and harmony among members, following frequent biblical injunctions and the model for unity seen in the Trinity, Father, Son and Holy Spirit, is the "soul of fellowship" for Christ's Body (p. 160).

Roman Catholics would find these various concepts of church familiar and acceptable, with the exception of his strong emphasis on small groups. So, too, would most other Christian denominations, e.g., Protestant traditions, or even Orthodox churches.

However, Catholics would be looking for more, like the teaching of the Holy Father in the 1940s, the momentous gathering of the bishops at the Second Vatican Council in the 1960s, and the massive *Catechism of the Catholic Church* in the 1990s.

Difference and Clarifications

✤ Catholic Church Family

In the 1940s, Pope Pius XII issued three encyclicals which were to serve as the foundation for many future developments in the Catholic Church during the second half of the last century.

One was on Sacred Scripture; a second on the Liturgy, and a third on the Mystical Body of Christ.

The last enlarged the notion of the Church which many Roman Catholics possessed at the time. The Church, the document taught, was not merely an organization with the pope, bishops, and priests, nor a system of rules and repetitions; nor was it simply a complex of buildings which included a church edifice, of course, but also schools, residences and hospitals.

The Church was and is more than these external visible components. It is a living, organic body, the *Mystical Body of Christ* in which all its members are by grace linked together and united in Christ.

Two biblical notions express that much richer notion of the Church.

The first, a rural and agricultural image, describes the Church in Jesus' words: "I am the vine, you are the branches" (John 15:1-10). There is thus an intimate communion between Christ and those who follow him; this means, consequently, that a close bond exists among his disciples as well, since they are linked together by such a common bond with Jesus.

> *. . . a living, organic body, the Mystical Body of Christ in which all its members are by grace linked together and united in Christ.*

The second, a more general image, views the Church as the Body of Christ with Jesus as the head and we the members. St. Paul in several places employs this notion: "As a body is one though it has many parts, and all the parts of the body, though many, are one body, so also Christ. For in one Spirit we were all baptized into one body . . . Now you are Christ's body, and individually parts of it. . . . If one part suffers, all the parts suffer with it; if one part is honored, all the parts share its joy" (1 Corinthians 12:12-31).

At the conversion of Saul to Paul on the road to Damascus we see dramatized this teaching on the Mystical Body of Christ. Saul, on his way to persecute Christians, encounters Jesus who questions him: "Saul, Saul, why are you persecuting me?" He replies, "Who are you, sir?" Christ responds: "I am Jesus, whom you are persecuting . . ." (Acts 9:1-9).

The bond between Christ and his followers is that close.

The Holy Spirit makes the Church the temple of the living God.

In the early 1960s, the bishops at the Second Vatican Council in their "Dogmatic Constitution on the Church," dedicated an entire chapter to the Church as *The People of God.* That image flows from words of God through the prophet Jeremiah: "I will be their God, and they will be my people" (Jeremiah 31:33).

All the faithful throughout the world make up this one people of God and are in communion with each other through the Holy Spirit.

In the 1990s, the *Catechism of the Catholic Church* describes the Church as People of God, Body of Christ, and Temple of the Holy Spirit.

The Holy Spirit makes the Church the temple of the living God. As an invisible principle, the Spirit joins all members together with one another and with their head, Christ the Lord.

The Church, then, is not simply a loosely connected group of people, but a spiritual family linked together by a real and unique, even though invisible bond.

✤ Power of the Sacraments

Pastor Warren states that "Baptism doesn't make you a member of God's family; only faith in Christ does that. Baptism shows you are a part of God's family" (Day 15).

Two decades ago there was a slight trend or movement in the Roman Catholic Church maintaining a view somewhat similar to Rick Warren's approach. It could be summarized in this way: The sacraments merely confirm something that has already happened. For example, the sacrament of Penance does not forgive sins; it simply celebrates that God has already forgiven the penitent person.

This approach never gained great momentum and ran into official opposition. The Church teaches that the sacraments require faith and their effectiveness depends upon the disposition of the recipient. However, it also insists that there is, in addition, a certain objective power in the sacraments themselves regardless of the personal holiness of the minister.

The *Catechism* summarizes this traditional teaching in these words:

> **1127** Celebrated worthily in faith, the sacraments confer the grace that they signify. They are

efficacious because in them Christ himself is at work: it is he who baptizes, he who acts in his sacraments in order to communicate the grace that each sacrament signifies. The Father always hears the prayer of his Son's Church which, in the epiclesis of each sacrament, expresses her faith in the power of the Spirit. As fire transforms into itself everything it touches, so the Holy Spirit transforms into divine life whatever is subjected to his power.

1128   This is the meaning of the Church's affirmation that the sacraments act *ex opere operato* (literally: "by the very fact of the action's being performed"), i.e., by virtue of the saving work of Christ, accomplished once for all. It follows that "the sacrament is not wrought by the righteousness of either the celebrant or the recipient, but by the power of God. From the moment that a sacrament is celebrated in accordance with the intention of the Church, the power of Christ and his Spirit acts in and through it, independently of the personal holiness of the minister. Nevertheless, the fruits of the sacraments also depend on the disposition of the one who receives them.

Affirmation and Enrichment

✤ Passover, Paschal or Easter Mystery

A central theme in the gospel is the notion of the Passover, Paschal or Easter mystery. That concept, in relationship to Christ, has a past, present and future dimension to it.

The *past* recalls Jewish deliverance from pagan bondage, their Passover from slavery to freedom, from the burdens and oppression of Egypt to the milk and honey of the Promised Land. This deliverance was achieved by blood (the lamb's blood sprinkled above the door signaling an angel of destruction to "pass over" that home). It was also accomplished by water (a miraculous parting of the Red Sea which enabled the Chosen People to "pass through" this wall of water, leaving the stricken Egyptian forces behind and opening the path to their new home.

The *present,* applied to Jesus, refers to his triple prediction of the Passover, or Paschal (similar terms) event ahead of him. He would with firm purpose make his way to Jerusalem, there to suffer and die, but rise. In undergoing these experiences, Christ would Passover from darkness to light, from death to life during this Good Friday through Easter Sunday experience. Jesus' own Passover, with the outpouring of blood and water from his side, will enable people for the

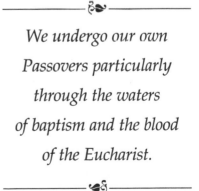

We undergo our own Passovers particularly through the waters of baptism and the blood of the Eucharist.

centuries ahead likewise to share through him their own similar Passover, Paschal or Easter journeys.

The *future* centers upon Christ continuing to work in our midst today, transforming us, moving us from sin and darkness to grace and life. We undergo our own Passovers particularly through the waters of baptism and the blood of the Eucharist.

A careful reading of the synoptic gospels (Matthew, Mark and Luke) reveals a fascinating pattern in Jesus' triple prediction of his Passover. Each one is preceded by a marvelous sign of Christ's power—multiplication of the loaves and fishes, the transfiguration, and the healing of sick persons. Then follows the prediction expressed three times, but in slightly different phrases. Finally, the Lord sketches three requirements, if we are to become his personal followers.

With a bible in one hand and some time to spare, a reader can follow in detail according to the outline below the scriptural sequence of this prediction.

Prediction #1

Marvelous Sign: Multiplication of Loaves and Fishes   Mt 14:13-21

Prediction: Mk 8:31

Lesson: Doctrine of the Cross   Lk 9:23

Prediction #2

Marvelous Sign: Transfiguration   Luke 9:28-36

Prediction: Mt 17:22-23

Lesson: Against Ambition and Envy   Mk 9:33-35; Mt 18:1-4

Prediction #3

Marvelous Sign: Healing the Crowds   Mt 19:1-2

Prediction: Mt 20:17-19

Lesson: Servants of Others   Mt 20:26-28

❖ Nature of Heaven

A recent survey indicated that over 70% of Americans believe in heaven, but hold extremely different views about the nature of the next world. Moreover, heaven, like all ultimate realities such as God, life and death, defies definition and is beyond human comprehension.

While acknowledging this limitation, we sketch some elements of heaven based upon several biblical texts, our liturgical rites and common Catholic traditions.

We stand before the *Divine Presence* and see God face to face. In doing so, we will find fulfilled our yearning for the timeless, for perfect happiness and for answers to all questions. In Eucharistic Prayer III we hear these words, based on 1 John 3:2, "On that day we shall see you, our God, as you are."

In heaven we will also be *reunited* with those who have gone before us. A commendation prayer at the conclusion of the Catholic funeral liturgy expresses this hope: "Open the gates of paradise to your servant and help us who remain to comfort one another with assurances of faith, until we all meet Christ and are with you and with our brother/sister for ever."

For the acutely suffering, terminally ill person and that individual's family, the vision of heaven in which there is *no pain or sorrow* can be tremendously consoling. The Book of Revelation describes the new heaven and new earth in this way: God "will wipe away every tear from their eyes, and there shall be no more death or mourning, wailing or pain . . ." (21:3-4).

The Apostles Creed expresses our belief in the Communion of Saints, that a *connection* continues after death between ourselves here on earth and those in heaven. The *Catholic Catechism* cites Saint Dominic and Saint Therese of Lisieux as examples of those in heaven interceding for us on earth. The latter, known as the Little Flower, promised: "I want to spend my heaven in doing good on earth."

> *"I want to spend my heaven in doing good on earth."*

Today we hear and read more frequently about people in this world supposedly connecting in some personal way with those who have died.

✤ Commandment of Love

Responding to an inquiry about which commandment is the greatest, Jesus cited two Old Testament texts: To love God and to love your neighbor (Mt 22:34-40; Mk 12:28-34).

The *Catechism* in its treatment of the ten command-
ments categorizes them according to Christ's response
to that question. The first three deal with the injunction
to love God with our whole
heart, soul and mind; the
other seven focus on the
requirement to love our
neighbor.

Some Catholic moral
theologians argue that it
is, practically speaking, impossible to lead a perfect
Christian life. This may
sound rather bizarre be-
cause the decalogue seems
doable enough.

. . . the very impossibility
to observe perfectly
Jesus' message simply
compels us always to
recognize our need for
God's strength and
forgiveness.

But when you add to those ten, the beatitudes, the
insistence upon forgiving others, and, perhaps most
critically, the challenge of Matthew 25 about responding or not responding to people in need, the argument
of these scholars gains credibility.

Such theologians, however, would conclude that the
very impossibility to observe perfectly Jesus' message
simply compels us always to recognize our need for
God's strength and forgiveness.

❖ Process of Forgiving

The need to let go of resentment and hurts is one
thing; how we can forgive those who, in our judgment
have wounded us, is another.

A missionary preacher lists four steps in the forgiving process, a procedure he learned over several years following a painful personal injury.

- Recognize that the person whom we judge hurt us had her or his reasons. They may have been wrong, false or erroneous motives. But few, if any people maliciously seek to wound or cause pain.

- Do not brood over the injury. That simply intensifies the hurt and leads to self-righteous ponderings.

- Distinguish between forgiving and feeling that we have forgiven someone. God insists that we forgive others, but knows we may never be able to forget the hurtful episode. Some torture themselves, judging that they have not forgiven another, as Christ commands, because they continue to experience ill feelings on occasion toward that person. Those are simply natural and understandable reactions or emotions which may linger on for life.

- Take a step toward forgiveness. This does not mean reconciliation with the person, a peaceful reuniting which may never be possible or ever occur. It does, however, require some move on our part to forgive, to let go. For example, a simple prayer each day for the specific individual, like an Our Father or Hail Mary, asking God to bless the other, gradually will soften our heart and allow bitterness to dissipate.

❖ Calumny and Detraction

A brief section in the *Catechism* about false witness and perjury should unsettle all of us, particularly a description of detraction **(2477)**.

We would probably recognize *calumny* as particularly evil and seek to avoid it at all costs. That occurs when we harm the reputation of others by saying not only bad, but also false and untrue things about them.

Detraction on the other hand, reveals, without an objectively valid reason, another's faults and failings to persons who do not know those negative elements about the individual.

Detraction seems to be a very common fault for all of us. During idle gossip or even friendly conversation, we easily share something negative about another, true, but bad information unknown to those with whom we are conversing. "Did you hear that so and so was fired or that so and so is no longer married or so and so has an addiction problem?"

❖ Self-giving

Pope John Paul II frequently taught that the human heart is restless unless it is self-giving.

The notion of love as self-giving is a very personal and dynamic concept.

Each day we face countless situations when we can respond in either a self-giving or self-centered fashion.

For example, we might hold the door for someone or impatiently jump ahead of others waiting in line.

Self-giving, however, sometimes entails allowing others to love or serve us. An ophthalmologist informed my nearly 70-year-old brother that he was now legally blind through macular degeneration. Today he can no longer drive, read the newspaper or study a restaurant menu. Self-giving requires that my brother at this point allows his wife to fulfill those functions for him.

Chapter 4

Becoming Like Christ

(Warren's Purpose #3:
"You Were Created to Become Like Christ" Days 22-28)

FOR Day 24, Pastor Rick Warren in his remarkable, staccato style supplies readers with a powerful, but not surprising aid in their journey to become like Christ. It is, of course, the Bible, which he argues is more than a doctrinal cookbook. In one of his book's finest passages, Warren details the power of God's word.

> God's Word generates life, creates faith, produces change, frightens the Devil, causes miracles, heals hurts, builds character, transforms circumstances, imparts joy, overcomes adversity, defeats temptation, infuses hope, releases power, cleanses our minds, brings things into being, and guarantees our future forever! We cannot live without the Word of God! Never take it for granted. You should consider it as essential to your life as food.

Roman Catholics could and most would say "Yes, Yes, Yes," to those statements. But they also know that there are significant differences in his and the Catholic approach to the Bible.

Differences and Clarifications

✤ Catholic and Protestant Bibles

During the past century it probably would be accurate to maintain that Catholic and Protestant bibles were different. The latter, following the reservations of some scholars, generally omitted seven Old Testament books called the Apocryphal or Deuterocanonical Books: Tobit, Judith, Wisdom, Sirach (Ecclesiasticus), Baruch, 1 and 2 Maccabees, and parts of Daniel and Esther.

In addition, Martin Luther rejected the New Testament books of Jude, Hebrews, James and Revelation.

All of these were included in Catholic Bibles and excluded from certain Protestant Bibles.

Today, however, many, perhaps most Bibles would include those disputed texts.

For example, *The Complete Parallel Bible* published by the Oxford University Press of New York notes in its title page "Containing The Old and New Testaments with the Apocryphal/Deuterocanonical Books" for the *New Revised Standard Version* and *Revised English Bible* (basically Protestant translations), and *New American Bible* and *New Jerusalem Bible* (both produced basically by Catholic scholars).

I am not sure where Pastor Warren stands on this point. As we have cited earlier, he quotes from 15 translations in his book, including the *New American Bible* and the *New Jerusalem Bible*.

Nevertheless, in quick glance at his notes (pages 327-334), I found reference to books rejected by Martin Luther, but none to the seven Apocryphal/Deutero-canonical books.

✤ Scripture Alone

The Protestant tradition, including evangelical churches, holds the "written down" phrases, the Bible itself, as the only official revelation of God's Word. I would imagine that Pastor Rick Warren would subscribe to that belief.

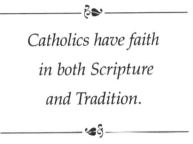

Catholics have faith in both Scripture and Tradition.

Roman Catholics, however, while holding the Bible in great reverence, seeing it as God's inspired word and using it at every worship service, believe also in the spoken word, the "handed down" oral tradition of the Church. Catholics have faith in both Scripture and Tradition.

The *Catechism of the Catholic Church* summarizes that teaching in these paragraphs:

> *One common source . . .*
>
> **80** Sacred Tradition and Sacred Scripture, then, are bound closely together and communicate one with the other. For both of them, flowing out from the same divine well-spring, come together in some fashion to form one thing and move

towards the same goal. Each of them makes present and fruitful in the Church the mystery of Christ, who promised to remain with his own "always, to the close of the age."

. . . two distinct modes of transmission

81   *Sacred Scripture* is the speech of God as it is put down in writing under the breath of the Holy Spirit. And [Holy] *Tradition* transmits in its entirety the Word of God which has been entrusted to the apostles by Christ the Lord and the Holy Spirit. It transmits it to the successors of the apostles so that, enlightened by the Spirit of truth, they may faithfully preserve, expound, and spread it abroad by their preaching.

—————— ࣰ ——————

Sacred Scripture is the speech of God as it is put down in writing under the breath of the Holy Spirit.

—————— ࣰ ——————

82   As a result the Church, to whom the transmission and interpretation of Revelation is entrusted, does not derive her certainty about all revealed truths from the holy Scriptures alone. Both Scripture and Tradition must be accepted and honored with equal sentiments of devotion and reverence.

97   Sacred Tradition and Sacred Scripture make up a single sacred deposit of the Word of God

(DV 10), in which, as in a mirror, the pilgrim Church contemplates God, the source of all her riches.

100   The task of interpreting the Word of God authentically has been entrusted solely to the Magisterium of the Church, that is, to the Pope and to the bishops in communion with him.

Affirmation and Enrichment

✤ **Fostering Relationships**

In developing and fostering relationships with Christ and with others, we need to keep in mind three points: by nature we are alone and know aloneness; because of human weakness we cannot totally avoid feelings of loneliness; self-giving love bridges the gaps created by our aloneness and can ease the pain caused by loneliness.

By our very nature we are alone, distinct individuals separated from all others. No one else has our fingerprints, DNA or, presumably, Social Security number. That *aloneness* manifests itself in several ways.

Decisions: While multiple factors may influence our thinking, our judgments and consequently our decision-making process, nevertheless only we can make the final choice—yes or no, do this or don't do that.

Temptations: Flip Wilson, in a long ago television series, made famous the remark "The devil made me do it." Again, a multiplicity of influences can weaken or minimize the power of our wills to resist temptations and therefore diminish our responsibility for certain actions or non-actions. Still, ultimately only we can choose to succumb or overcome a temptation.

Death: It is highly desirable to have someone who cares about us by our side, to touch or even hold us when we die. Regardless, we must pass through that portal from here to eternity alone. Only we personally experience our own deaths.

God: Father Henri Nouwen's mother lived a saintly life. Yet this valiant, spiritual woman told her son that she feared facing the all-holy God and showing the Divine Lord her sins. Such reluctance would surprise others who knew Mrs. Nouwen as a very saintly lady. However, the closer we are to light, the clearer our darkness becomes; similarly the closer we are to God, the clearer our own creature status, sin prone nature stands out. This woman, with that clarity of vision, knew she must face God alone.

Disappointments and Grief: When major disappointments or family deaths enter our lives, we usually can count on the presence of at least several persons to support us. Huge lines at funeral homes for calling hours and a substantial number of consoling notes are clear illustrations of that phenomenon. But as time moves on, so does life and the disappointed or grieving person is left to cope alone.

Roman Catholics, however, are spiritually never totally alone. They can find support through their belief in a Guardian Angel, the Holy Trinity, the link with other members of the Church as the Mystical Body of Christ and the People of God.

Because of human weakness we cannot totally avoid *loneliness*. Loneliness, however, is a feeling, an emotion, and by nature undulating, wave-like, ebbing and flowing, rising and falling, coming and going.

The image of a ship moving through some large body of water and churning up a series of substantial waves may clarify that statement. When the waves finally make their way to the shore, experienced swimmers know how to dive through them. They can feel the powerful crash of the wave just beyond their feet, yet realize that the water will soon subside, allowing them to reach the surface and the welcome air.

However, inexperienced swimmers, neither skilled at diving through the waves nor understanding that the water will shortly subside, may frantically flail in a vain attempt to reach the surface. Their frenetic efforts only make things worse, even sometimes leading to disastrous consequences.

An awareness of the wave-like nature of feelings, including loneliness and grief accompanying deep personal losses, can help us. We may then better grasp that eventually the emotion will subside, allowing us to breathe again and we simply let the wave flow over us.

We cannot avoid aloneness because of our very nature or loneliness because of our weak human condition. But *love* helps us connect with others, to bridge the gap as it were through relationships and may also greatly mitigate the occasions and intensity of loneliness.

Love defies a definition, but the concept that love essentially entails self-giving captures its main thrust. The opposite of love would be self-centeredness.

Each day presents us with a series of opportunities for either a self-giving or a self-getting response. For example, someone with an inner burden may wish to visit with us about it. In a self-giving way, we may immediately share some of our precious time to listen or, in a self-getting manner, decline to talk because of our busy schedule.

Pope John Paul II frequently proclaimed that the human heart is not content unless it is self-giving.

Pope John Paul II frequently proclaimed that the human heart is not content unless it is self-giving.

It should be noted, nevertheless, that there are situations when true love may require someone to allow others to love or serve him. That often occurs when people are seriously ill or disabled.

✤ Positive Coincidences

The refrain for a Responsorial Psalm at Mass pleads with God, "Let us see your kindness and we shall be saved." In other words, help us to recognize your

Divine Presence in the events of our everyday lives.

We see this demonstrated in the fascinating story of that troubled prophet Elijah (1 Kings 19:1-15). God tells him to go outside the cave on the mountainside and "The Lord will be passing by." There was subsequently a strong heavy wind, an earthquake and a fire. But the Lord was not in any of these. Eventually, however, God spoke to the prophet through a tiny whispering sound.

Several years ago James Redfield's novel *The Celestine Prophesy* reached the bestseller list. Early on in the characters' search for insights, they become conscious of coincidences in their lives, events which happen not simply out of pure chance but "guided by some unexplained force," experiences which induce a sense of mystery, excitement and life (pp. 6-7).

We might express it in this way: Positive coincidences in our lives can lead us to transcendence, to an awareness of the Divine Presence in daily occurrences.

During World War II, a married physician was missing in action during battles for the Pacific Islands. His wife began a novena, nine days of prayer honoring Saint Therese, the Little Flower, who had promised while on earth that, once in heaven, she would send roses as a sign of God's response to prayer.

The physician's wife lived in a predominantly Jewish neighborhood. Several days into the novena, a neighbor knocked on the door bearing a gift for her. Her Jewish friend knew nothing about a novena, the

Little Flower or the roses. But she presented the physician's spouse with a dozen red roses.

Shortly thereafter her husband was found safe and sound. To the end of her life she saw in those roses a sign of God's special, loving Presence.

❖ Read the Bible and Memorize Verses

Pastor Rick Warren reminds us that if we read the Bible just fifteen minutes a day, we will cover all of it once a year. He also lists some of the benefits of memorizing Bible verses. That practice will "help you resist temptation, make wise decisions, reduce stress, build confidence, offer good advice and share your faith with others" (pp. 188-189).

There are somewhat parallel comments to his advice in the Catholic tradition.

When the Church introduced its new Lectionary for Catholic worship a need emerged for trained lectors to proclaim assigned texts in the vernacular. A religious educator, liturgist and theologian published a list of 25 suggestions for these readers' preparation process. Three of them were identical: *read the Bible every day.*

The late Henri J.M. Nouwen, an enormously popular author and speaker on spirituality, once described his own prayer pattern. Before retiring he would read the biblical texts for the next day's Mass (the Lectionary provides the specific readings for both Sundays and Weekdays). From those passages, Nouwen would select a word, phrase or image that resonated with him. As he awaited sleep, or was awakened in the middle of his rest, this author would recall that word, phrase or image. It thus became a kind of sacred icon offering him a safe and sacred refuge when, in his words, he might be tempted to idolatry. The next day, during his regular hour of meditative prayer, Nouwen would return to that excerpt from the Bible as the starting point for his reflection.

- In *Slow Down* a small book of 100 five-minute meditations for de-stressing one's day which is outlined in the Appendix, and *Take Five* its sequel, each reflection has a relevant phrase or sentence from the Bible to be carried within a person's mind and heart throughout the day.

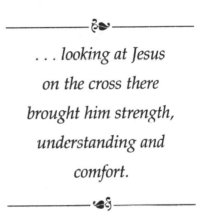

. . . looking at Jesus on the cross there brought him strength, understanding and comfort.

❖ **Eyes Fixed on Jesus**

Becoming like Christ means, in words of the Letter to the Hebrews, "Keeping our eyes fixed on Jesus, the leader and perfecter of faith" (Hebrews 12:1).

- The late Bishop Joseph O'Keefe, former bishop of the Syracuse diocese and native New Yorker, took that phrase for his episcopal motto: *Respice ad Jesum* "Keep your eyes fixed on Jesus."

- Father Kevin Murphy, a priest of our diocese, died at the early age of 33, suffering greatly and ultimately dying from cancer. Next to his hospital bed he had placed a large crucifix and found looking at Jesus on the cross there brought him strength, understanding and comfort.

- Pope John XXIII likewise found Christ on the cross a constant source of inspiration. Before getting into bed, he knelt before the crucifix hanging on the wall, immediately saw it if he awakened at night, and was the first image before his eyes upon arising. The cross, he said, is the primary sign of God's love for us.

> *The cross, he said,*
>
> *is the primary sign*
>
> *of God's love*
>
> *for us.*

✤ Temptations

Christ was like us in all ways except sin. He was tempted, at the beginning of his ministry and in the Garden of Gethsemane at the end. He clearly conquered, overcame, and successfully resisted these temptations.

That example should help us understand the critical difference between sin and temptation. Sin occurs when we freely and knowingly fail to follow the divine imperative within us. Temptation, however

strong and violent it may be, is not a sin unless we succumb to it.

Some leaders in the past have neglected to distinguish between sin and temptation as well as between
serious sin (e.g. murder or adultery) and lesser sin
(e.g. minor impatience or impulsive words). Failure
to make those distinctions will cause havoc in our
spiritual lives.

Many contemporary people struggle with addictions, overwhelming temptations to misuse such
things as alcohol, drugs, sex and food.

To overcome such addictions one must resist denial
and admit a problem exists. Then the following steps,
observed faithfully, can lead to control of the addiction
and a healthy management of one's life.

- The addiction is not your fault. Therefore, don't
  punish yourself with guilt or blame yourself
  that you have it.

- The addiction will never go away. You can
  become a *recovering* addict, never a recovered
  addict.

- Using the means available (like a 12-step program) can make it possible for you to control
  the addiction and bring a peaceful order to your
  life.

- Observe the HALT warnings: be conscious that
  being too *hungry, angry, lonely* or *tired* makes
  you vulnerable to the addiction's pull.

- Without a power beyond yourself, God, it is impossible to manage or bring the addiction under control.

Becoming like Christ also means depending on Jesus to lead us, sustain us, and lift us up when we falter.

Chapter 5

God's Servant

(Warren's Purpose # 4:
"You Were Shaped for Serving God" Days 29-35)

IN recent years, *Servant Leadership* has been both a best-seller book and popular concept. Good leaders, it maintains, serve others. In Purpose # 4 Rick Warren with his powerful and practical style develops that notion. His words about time and talent will resonate well with Roman Catholics who have grown accustomed to Stewardship, Volunteer or Ministry Sundays, with their appeal to share one's gifts in the service of others. His teaching on tithing, however, has been neither universally taught nor accepted in most Catholic parishes.

We mentioned earlier in this book our wonderment about Warren's words that we will be reunited in heaven with loved ones who are believers. Does he mean to exclude those who are not believers? A parallel exists with his repeated remarks about serving others who are believers. Does he limit service to believers?

Differences and Clarifications

✤ Tithing

Rick Warren, speaking to business persons, urges them to "return at least a tithe (10%) of the profit to God as an act of worship" (Day 31).

He cites in support of his words the Deuteronomy passage about tithing (Deuteronomy 14: 22-29). In addition, the Saddleback pastor refers to the prophet Malachi's words: "Bring the whole tithe into the storehouse . . ." (Malachi 3:8-11).

During the 1960s a special committee for the U.S. bishops studied the question of tithing in the Catholic Church. They concluded that the practice, while appropriate as an ideal, was not legally binding upon Catholics, that the current division of the 10%—into half for the parish and half for all other charities—was acceptable, and that the tithing approach in over a thousand U.S. parishes had proven very beneficial from a pastoral viewpoint.

There were at that time a few advocates for tithing among Catholic leaders in this country, but no general or universal support of the practice.

My own initiation came in the 1970s through a remarkable layman from Detroit, "Giggs" Lenzi who, as a volunteer, visited upon request over 300 parishes in the nation and effectively preached the tithing message.

His approach in our parish immediately raised the Sunday collection from $1,750 to $3,500. That success eventually led me to train a few lay speakers to introduce the concept to over one hundred parishes in our diocese (with an average growth in Sunday offerings of 45%), and to publish nationally several materials to be used for explaining and implementing this Sacrificial Giving Process.

I then met Dutch and Barbara Scholtz, a couple who had tithed for 20 years, and together we promoted Sacrificial Giving around the nation. They developed a corps of speakers and have now facilitated introduction of tithing into over 2,000 Catholic parishes in the United States, with the average growth rate in Sunday offerings again to be approximately 45%.

In 1992, the National Conference of Catholic Bishops published a pastoral letter on the subject, *Stewardship: A Disciple's Response*. While it briefly acknowledges the tradition of tithing as an expression of stewardship, the document follows more of the high road, as it were, with general theological and spiritual principles about sharing our gifts in response to God's call.

Monsignor Thomas McCread, pastor of a Kansas parish, has preached for decades on time, talent and treasure including the biblical notion of tithing. His remarkable success over the years in that church gained him national recognition as well as support from the U.S. bishops to promote his concept.

The concept of stewardship has now become more commonly accepted and taught in Catholic churches throughout the United States. However, the specific recommendations of tithing do not enjoy that same acceptance; proportionate giving is instead the more general suggestion.

Relatively recent surveys indicate that few Americans and fewer Catholics tithe. For example in the 1960s Protestants gave 2.2% of their income to their

churches; Catholics gave about the same. More recently Protestants have remained at the same level;
Catholics have dipped to 1.1%.

Other examples: only 10% of Americans gave more
than 5% to charitable causes (their churches and charities). People making $100,000 or more led in charitable
giving, but were at only 3.2%. A study of denomina-
tional giving showed Latter Day Saints at the top with
nearly 7%; Catholics at the bottom with about 1.2%.

Tithing is preached and practiced more today in
Catholic Churches then in the last century. However,
its acceptance and implementation is still rather minimal.

❖ Believers Only

Earlier we described Rick Warren's statement that
we will meet believers in heaven. Did he and does he
mean only believers, only those who actually accept
Jesus as their Savior?

The issue arises again with regard to service of others. Pastor Warren, in this section, states:

"You need to be connected to a church family... to
fulfill your calling to serve other believers . . ." (p. 230).

"These are special God-empowered abilities for
serving him that are given only to believers" (p.236).

"Our weaknesses also encourage fellowship among
believers" (p. 275).

We could interpret those statements strictly to mean
serving believers only and not reaching out to others in

need. However, his own vision for eliminating poverty in Africa and the actual service efforts of the
Saddleback Community would seem to indicate that
those remarks are about emphasis rather than exclu-
sion.

In any event, Roman Catholics believe in and act out
of a special bond both with parishioners and also with
other Catholics throughout the world.

For example, most churches feature coffee and
donuts after Sunday Masses, parish picnics, and lun-
cheons for the bereaved following funeral services.

Moreover, the sacraments of baptism and anointing
of the sick have connections with the universal
Church; at each Mass the priest prays explicitly for the
current pope and the local bishop(s); annual collections
aid various local, national and international agencies to
carry out their ministries.

While there is, therefore, this bondedness among
Catholic believers, parishes take seriously the gospel
message of reaching out to anyone in need.

To illustrate: Catholic schools in center city often
have student bodies 75% of which come from below
poverty level income homes and 80% of which are not
Roman Catholic; an East Coast Cathedral Downtown
Emergency Service provides both ample food and pro-
fessional advocacy to many regardless of ethnic or religious backgrounds; a West Coast Cathedral provides a
soup kitchen which serves a hot meal daily to around
200 people with no questions asked.

Affirmation and Enrichment

✤ Qualities of Love

Purposes #2-4, *Formed for God's Family, Becoming Like Christ* and *Serving God Through Others* all involve love. Love is behind relationships in the church family, our link with Jesus, and carrying out the command to serve others.

Love is behind relationships in the church family, our link with Jesus, and carrying out the command to serve others.

We earlier have described love as self-giving which sometimes includes allowing other people to give to us. Here are four more specific qualities of love, concepts originally proposed by Eric Fromm in *The Art of Loving*.

- *Care and Concern.* These words have a particular meaning in this context: to see, develop and actualize the potential in another person or other people. President Lincoln, as described in Doris Kearns Goodwin's masterful study, *Team of Rivals,* had that loving gift of care and concern.

Some years ago, a leadership book, *Search for Excellence* suggested several steps for praising or affirming people—another manifestation of care and concern: reward people for good work immediately, on the spot; be specific in your

praise; remember that a leader's words or ges-
tures possess special power; affirm individuals
frequently, but irregularly, lest the affirmation
become routine.

- *Responsive.* Empathetic would be a synonym for
this quality of love. Walking in people's shoes;
feeling their feelings. Attentive listening to another is the essential ingredient to responsiveness;
so, too, is keeping one's focus on the other and
not on ourselves.

- *Respect.* This quality would have us take people
as they are, not as we want them to be or as they
should be. That seems to be the key ingredient to
all successful relationships. There is a corollary to
respect: we can only be upset by others to the
extent we allow them to upset us. Allowing this
to happen gives others power over our inner
selves, which is not a healthy situation.

- *Understanding.* People who love practice understanding; they go beneath the surface of others'
actions and ask why. One psychologist finds that
the better he gets to know his patients or clients,
the more he comes to like them. In going beneath
the surface, he discovers the richness of their lives.

❖ Reluctant Servants

Pastor Warren, in another of his masterful, staccato-
like comments, describes how God used quite a variety
of misfits for divine service (Day 29, p. 233).

Abraham was old, Jacob was insecure, Leah was unattractive, Joseph was abused, Moses stuttered, Gideon was poor, Samson was codependent, Rahab was immoral, David had an affair and all kinds of family problems, Elijah was suicidal, Jeremiah was depressed, John was reluctant, Naomi was a widow, John the Baptist was eccentric to say the least, Peter was impulsive and hot-tempered, Martha worried a lot, the Samaritan woman had several failed marriages, Zacchaeus was unpopular, Thomas had doubts, Paul had poor health, and Timothy was timid.

When I became rector at the Cathedral in Syracuse ten years ago, a parish leader told me that people who attend this church do not want to be involved. That probably was understandable. Few members actually live within the territorial boundaries; they love this century old large structure with its high ceiling, stained-glass windows and superb music; these parishioners want fine services, but also guard their anonymity.

That negative reaction was, however, disturbing and distressing for me. My basic theological and pastoral approach included the maximum involvement of members in parish life. The resistance I encountered seemed to parallel the hesitation of those biblical people named by Rick Warren.

Nevertheless, I am delighted to add that two years of teaching and preaching on the subject as well as individual and group invitations to participate in various activities gradually altered that situation.

An annual Volunteer Weekend now consistently brings forth over a hundred new persons offering their gifts for building up the church and making this a better world. That number pales in comparison to the several thousand volunteer servants in larger parishes (7,000 in Saddleback Church), but for the Cathedral it signals a dramatic shift in attitudes (Day 31, p. 244).

❖ Grateful Caretaking

The seven days under Purpose # 4 deal with different dimensions of being God's servants, doing the work which God gave us to do.

In Roman Catholic circles a similar or parallel thrust would be termed Stewardship, Sacrificial Giving or, in a newer approach, Grateful Caretakers of God's Many Gifts.

That last concept finds its basis in the Bible, the liturgy and, the official teaching of the Catholic Church.

Grateful Caretaking looks to the two *biblical creation stories*—Genesis 1:28 and 2:15. God displays to our ancestors the good and wonderful world before them, then commands our ancestors to "fill the earth and subdue it" and "to cultivate and care for it." In other words, be responsible caretakers of all of God's creation.

Two liturgical prayers mention that *"every good thing comes from God"* and that God is "the source of life and goodness" (Opening Prayer, 22nd Sunday in Ordinary Time and Eucharistic Prayer IV).

Official teaching reminds us that it is a duty and honor to *give back to God* a portion of the goods received from the Creator, (Second Vatican Council, *Decree on the Apostolate of the Laity:* Article 10). Three decades later, the *Catechism of the Catholic Church* similarly stresses "the goods of creation are destined for the whole human race" (Article 2405).

This biblical, liturgical and official teaching presupposes three inner qualities for appropriate grateful caretaking.

Faith: To recognize that everything is a gift from God.

Gratitude: An awareness of these gifts quite naturally prompts or should prompt a grateful spirit within us.

Openness of Heart: This presumes a willingness to share a part of what we have received—time, talent and treasure—for making this a better world and building up the Church.

The American bishop's document, *Stewardship: A Disciple's Response,* summarizes these concepts in this way.

> Disciples who practice stewardship recognize God as the origin of life, the giver of freedom, the source of all they have and are and will be... They know themselves to be recipients and caretakers of God's many gifts. They are grateful for what they have received and eager to cultivate their

gifts out of love for God and one another (Paragraph 1).

The text defines a steward as:

One who receives God's gifts gratefully, cherishes and tends them in a responsible and accountable manner, shares them in justice and love with others, and returns them with increase to the Lord (Paragraph 7).

❖ Time, Talent and Treasure

Rick Warren in these seven days or chapters provides rich insights for leaders who wish to stimulate a spirit of Christian service to those among their flock. His pages no doubt will also motivate members to share their many gifts with others who may not be believers.

Stewardship advocates and Roman Catholic pastors tend to break down the gifts to be shared into time, talent and treasure.

Time. In today's busy world this may be the most precious commodity, the hardest gift to share. Time for us on earth, we know, is limited, fleeting and unpredictable.

In our inner city's, grades K-6 Catholic School, with a predominantly AfroAmerican, nonCatholic, below poverty level student body, two dozen mentors spend one hour each week with the same child for the entire year. These include people from diverse backgrounds, a half dozen *Oasis* volunteers and seven Syracuse

University students. They are sharing their time to give some boys and girls in need a better chance at life and a brighter future.

Talent. Our talents represent a combination of gifts received at birth, formed by education and enriched by experience. It is rather incredible to consider that jazz artist Dave Brubeck, in his eighties, still practices, composes, and performs.

Treasure. The treasure we possess may come from a salary, retirement income, social security check, part-time job, dividends, allowance, inheritance, or windfall. Grateful Caretaking holds up this ideal with regard to treasure: Give back to the Lord in gratitude or share of the treasure you had received; let it be a sacrifice, with a bite to it, offered during the worship service; use your church envelopes; look to the biblical ideal of a tithe, 5% for your parish and 5% for all other charities.

Many or most Catholic parishes schedule a weekend for soliciting time and talent and another weekend for treasure. Those experiences will include pertinent readings, appropriate music, witness talks, and literature as well as an opportunity to sign up for various service projects and make a financial commitment.

❖ A Messy Church

In Day 35, Pastor Warren speaks about "God's Power in Your Weakness." In an intriguing way he describes human frailty and the fact that this exists in each member of the church family.

Roman Catholics are well aware of the frail, weak nature of the church's members. Acceptance of that humanness has been especially difficult in recent years with the sexual abuse situations. Still, Catholics continue to believe in the Divine Presence within their church.

A knowledge of the Catholic Church's long history is helpful here. Many examples from the past exemplify its human and divine nature.

Catholics continue to believe in the Divine Presence within their church.

An English historian, not Roman Catholic, once uttered a famous comment that if any other human institution had known such great inner corruption or outer oppression, it would long ago have perished. For him, the Catholic Church's very survival is almost proof of its divine protection.

A well-regarded Catholic priest historian said that his greatest sense of hope, next to a belief in God's promise to Peter about being with the Church until the end of time, is his knowledge of the history of the Catholic Church.

I cited those words and examples to a group of worried priests some years ago and observed an immediate, noticeable reduction in their anxiety, a calmness descending upon them. They know well that the Catholic Church is a "messy" human group and, in a sense, regret that fact. But they also believe that the Holy Spirit in mysterious ways guides, corrects and supports the Church.

Chapter 6

Bringing the Message to Others

(Warren's Purpose #5:
"You Were Made for a Mission" Days 36-40)

MOST Roman Catholics would have no disagreement with Pastor Rick Warren's final section about our mission to bring Jesus' message of good news to others. However, they might find the intensity of his words quite unfamiliar, making them even somewhat uncomfortable.

Disagreements and Clarification

Warren, in defining and describing the word mission, sees ministry as a service to believers and mission as a service to unbelievers (Day 36).

Two terms come to mind to describe those who both believe in Christ and bring his message to others: disciples and apostles.

Disciples are those who listen and follow Jesus; apostles are those who have been sent by him to proclaim the gospel to the whole world.

The former baptistry of the Syracuse Cathedral contains an exceptionally creative and attractive mosaic on both side walls with a biblical quote over the entrance.

On one wall, the Risen Christ stands surrounded by two trees filled with birds, fruit and butterflies—all signs of life.

On the opposite wall, the eleven apostles stand in transfixed state with a dove, font and fish at the center of the mosaic.

Over the entrance are Matthew's words commissioning the disciples: "Go, therefore, and make disciples of all nations, baptizing in the name of the Father, and of the Son and of the Holy Spirit . . ." (Matthew 28:16-20).

Note that there were only eleven apostles. This was a post-resurrection appearance of Christ; Judas had taken his life; the apostles had not yet selected a successor; therefore, eleven instead of twelve.

These apostles were now, again, being sent out, commissioned, commanded to carry out a mission.

As Pastor Warren mentions, the word mission traces its origin to a Latin verb, *"Mitto . . . missum"* meaning send, sending, sent.

The dismissal phrase of the Mass in Latin is, *"Ite missa est,"* translated currently as the "Mass is ended, go in peace."

The term mission, then, is not unfamiliar to Roman Catholics. We employ the word commonly for such activities as missionary projects, parish missions, and missionary collections.

Rick Warren relates the touching story of his father, a preacher for over 50 years, mostly in small parishes, whose passion was to build tiny churches in "missionary" areas beyond our borders. Even though he oversaw the construction of 150 during his life, Warren's father, over his final days before succumbing to cancer, kept repeating "One more for Jesus." Whether he meant an individual soul or a church structure is not clear. But eventually during those last moments he laid a hand upon his son's head and repeated that phrase.

The Saddleback pastor obviously has matched his preacher father's missionary enthusiasm.

While the typical Roman Catholic priest or parishioner might not mirror that same intense mission spirit, the Church in general and local parishes in particular are very supportive of missionary efforts.

- The Vatican office for the Propagation of the Faith directs, encourages and supports missions and missionaries worldwide.
- Each fall, every parish in the United States takes up a second or special collection to help fund the work of those missionaries.
- Probably all dioceses in this country also participate in a "Missionary Cooperative Plan" which each year assigns to every parish a missionary speaker for one specific weekend.
- U.S. mission communities, like Maryknoll, send clergy and lay missionaries around the world to bring the good news to faraway places.
- An increasing number of dioceses and parishes adopt or partner with churches in developing countries, providing them with financial, material and personnel support.

These efforts pale in comparison to Pastor Warren's vision of the 500 small groups at Saddleback Church adopting individual Rwandan villages. Nor do most Catholics share the intensity of his mission dedication. Nevertheless, they are undertaking many activities of a missionary nature, even if there remains great room for growth and development.

✤ End of World

Roman Catholics are very skeptical of those prophets who in ominous terms predict the imminent coming of Christ and the end of this world as we know it.

Warren likewise rejects these prophecies and cites two biblical texts in support of his position (pp. 285-286).

In Acts 1:7-8, the apostles, just prior to the Ascension, asked Jesus: "Lord, are you at this time going to restore the Kingdom of Israel?" Christ responded: "It is not for you to know the times or seasons that the Father has established by his own authority."

In Matthew 24:36, Jesus said: "But of that day and hour no one knows, neither the angels of heaven, nor the Son, but the Father alone."

As Barclay, the famous Protestant biblical scholar observes, if Christ himself does not know the day or the hour, why should we mortal human beings expect to have that knowledge.

Catholics would applaud this explanation. However, Warren goes on to stress that Jesus will not return until the gospel has been preached to all the nations. "Then the end will come" (Matthew 24:14).

The false expectation of an imminent end should not, according to Pastor Warren, be used as an excuse to avoid mission efforts. On the other hand, Christ's words about when the end will come, should motivate believers to greater missionary endeavors.

Agreement and Affirmation

❖ **Personal Testimonies**

Rick Warren is a strong advocate of personal testimonies, understanding their power to convince and influence people. He also offers good guidance in helping people reflect upon and develop these kind of individualized stories (Day 37).

Here is his suggested framework for a testimony:

1. What my life was like before I met Jesus
2. How I realized I needed Jesus
3. How I committed my life to Jesus
4. The difference Jesus has made in my life

Then Warren offers some thought-provoking questions to jog people's memories and help to get them started in developing testimonies:

- What has God taught me from failure?
- What has God taught me from lack of money?
- What has God taught me from pain or sorrow or depression?
- What has God taught me through waiting?
- What has God taught me through illness?
- What has God taught me from disappointment?
- What have I learned from my family, my church, my relationships, my small group, and my critics?

There has been a gradual growth in the use of personal testimonies at Catholic services and events.

➤ An essential part of presenting "Grateful Caretaking of God's Many Gifts" is the testimony of lay witnesses who have taken a step in faith, begun tithing and, as a result, experienced peace and joy.

➤ At sessions of the Rite of Christian Initiation of Adults, each class often includes the testimony of a person who became Roman Catholic some years earlier.

➤ On Volunteer, Stewardship or Ministry Weekends, parishes frequently request persons to speak about how their participation in this or that activity has influenced them positively.

➤ Those in Catholic Charismatic Renewal groups expect and applaud testimonies from different persons about their spiritual journeys.

➤ Those in twelve-step groups welcome the testimonies of people struggling with addictions.

➤ A spirituality which includes theological reflection, "Lord, let us see your kindness and we shall be saved," recommends that participants recognize the presence of God in their daily lives. That procedure in turn generates excellent material for future personal testimonies.

✤ World Class or Global Vision

It is an obvious truth that we now live in a one world and global market society. A visit to New York

City, a check of where manufactured items are made, and a glance at CNN instantly reveal the oneness of our world.

Rick Warren applies that current reality to his emphasis on world class mission efforts (Day 38).

I have cited his desire to link Saddleback small groups to individual Rwandan churches. However, his vision is more expansive than that. He is thinking of an immense and universal volunteer effort, the PEACE plan, "transforming 400,000 churches in 47 nations into centers to nurse, feed and educate the poor and even turn them into entrepreneurs." (*Time*, August 22, 2005, p. 59).

The Catholic Church in the United States has been about such efforts to assist those in developing countries for decades, although on a perhaps less grandiose scale.

A visit to New York City, a check of where manufactured items are made, and a glance at CNN instantly reveal the oneness of our world.

- The World Mission Society (Propagation of Faith) once provided a colorful rosary and suggested that those using it dedicate each decade of prayer for a different continent.

- Others recommended that they pray each decade for a different country.

- An annual Lenten collection with its Rice Bowl component for Catholic Relief Services produces very substantial funds to assist people in developing countries help themselves. The Rice Bowl element combines prayer, fasting and works of charity, plus education, with a focus upon people and places beyond our borders.

- Some parishes tithe on their weekly offerings, placing 10% of the collection into a fund that will, on a quarterly basis, be distributed equally to groups in need outside the parish, the diocese and the country. Those parishes encourage the recipients to respond with information and photos for eventual display on a World Mission Board in their church entrances.

- The weekend General Intercessions or Prayer of the Faithful at Mass does or should mention consistently the concerns of the worldwide or global church.

✤ Small Groups and Journal Keeping

In his Day 39, Pastor Warren encourages, among other ways to balance one's life, small group participation and keeping a spiritual journal.

He states that the best way to internalize the principles of *The Purpose Driven Life* is "to discuss them with others in a *small-group setting*. In that way, they can give and receive feedback, discuss real-life examples, pray for, encourage and support each other as they live out these principles (pp. 306-307).

For Catholics, the small group concept began during recent times in Central and South America. It later surfaced in an adapted form through the RENEW process. That New Jersey based organization early on promoted these small group experiences in many U.S. parishes and dioceses as well as, now, overseas. After RENEW ended, there was some carry-over of the small group system in parishes, but not on a huge scale.

Nevertheless, today many Catholic Church leaders consider the small group process as a key to the revitalization of parish life throughout the United States.

. . . today many Catholic Church leaders consider the small group process as a key to the revitalization of parish life throughout the United States.

Warren also strongly recommends keeping a *spiritual journal*. That process reinforces our progress, records life lessons we don't wish to forget, helps us to remember valuable insights, clarifies our thinking and solidifies our resolutions (pp. 308-309).

A friend of mine, as a product of his Marriage Encounter experience, has been keeping a prayer journal for at least two decades. He faithfully spends about ten minutes each day recording his spiritual thoughts. That regular practice no doubt has produced the kind of positive results which Warren predicted.

Moving On

The journey of 40 days is now over, but in a sense it has just begun. With the reading, prayer reflection and perhaps group sharing, you very likely recognize some spiritual transformation within you which points to the future. A changed way of living beckons. However, given the weakness of our human nature, we may easily falter, stumble, even slip back into former patterns.

——————— ঌ ———————

A changed way of living beckons.

——————— ঌ ———————

The ideal, of course, is to keep God at the center of our lives. When we do, we worship; when we don't, we worry (Day 40, p. 314).

In concluding this book, I offer the words of four well-known persons, including Rick Warren, to help us keep God at the center of our lives:

Blessed Mother Teresa of Calcutta. Asked how she buried 40,000 people in her life, the saintly woman simply replied, "One by one. I picked up one dead person in the street, and then another, and another. One by one."

Did she ever feel overwhelmed by the enormous challenges before her—the abandoned infants, persons afflicted with AIDS, the feeble elderly? Her response: "You can only do what you can do."

Is there a key to right living? "It is not what you do that is important, but the amount of love you put into the doing."

Jean Valjean. The Christ-like heroic central figure in the musical *Les Miserables,* after a life of great pain and remarkable charity, knelt down before the silver candlesticks and crucifix given to him by a holy bishop. Knowing death was near, he prayed that God on high would take him, bring him home.

The musical concludes with a white-clad chorus welcoming Jean Valjean to heaven as they sing, "to love another person is to see the face of God."

Pastor Rick Warren. The *Good News Paper* is published by the Son Light Ministries, a not-for-profit agency that has been distributing 25,000 copies monthly free of charge in the Central New York area. Funded mainly by donations, it has been appearing in various supermarkets and other similar locations for nine years. Its May 2006 issue contained an interview with Rick Warren. This is an excerpt from "Thoughts by Rick Warren."

> This past year has been the greatest year of my life but also the toughest, with my wife, Kay, getting cancer.
>
> I used to think that life was hills and valleys— you go through a dark time, then you go to the mountaintop, back and forth. I don't believe that anymore.
>
> Rather than life being hills and valleys, I believe that it's kind of like two rails on a railroad track, and at all times you have something good and something bad in your life.

No matter how good things are in your life, there is always something bad that needs to be worked on.

And no matter how bad things are in your life, there is always something good you can thank God for.

At the end of the interview, Pastor Warren offers five practice points:

Happy moments, PRAISE GOD.

Difficult moments, SEEK GOD.

Quiet moments, WORSHIP GOD.

Painful moments, TRUST GOD.

Every moment, THANK GOD.

Blessed Pope John XXIII. At 76 most people have retired or anticipate doing so in the near future. That was not to be the case for Angelo Roncalli, the short and stocky, but cheerful and wise Patriarch of Venice. In somewhat of a surprise, he was elected on October 28, 1958 as the next Holy Father of the Catholic Church and took his new name, Pope John XXIII.

He became famous for brief and sometimes humorous comments. "Holy Father, how many people work in the Vatican?" "About half of them."

However, he had remarkable vision, once saying, "We are not on earth as museum keepers but to cultivate a flourishing garden of life and to prepare a glorious future" (Thomas Cahill, *Pope John XXIII*, p. 158).

This elderly man convened the Second Vatican Council, a four-year gathering of bishops from around the world, which was to change quite radically the Catholic Church for the next half century.

But Pope John XXIII was a prayerful person with a profound trust in God.

It is said of him that at night before retiring he slipped into the chapel and prayed. One would presume that with his advanced age and many burdens, this interval of prayerful meditation extended for a lengthy period of time.

"Lord, it is your church.

I am going to bed."

Pope John XXIII

Not so.

Supposedly, this Holy Father looked up at the altar and simply said, "Lord, it is your church. I am going to bed."

That example serves as a model for us as we leave Pastor Rick Warren with his inspirational forty days and move into the future applying those lessons learned to our own lives.

Appendix

Spirituality and Stress

IN the Introduction to this book, I mentioned two sessions, one in the fall of 2005 and another in the spring of 2006, entitled "Developing A Purpose Driven and Stress Free Life."

The groups (40 in one and 100 in the other) met six times, once each week for 90 minutes for biblical reflective prayer, group sharing and my extended reflections on both *The Purpose Driven Life* and my own small book, *Slow Down.* Written evaluations after each were very positive.

The major portion of this publication, *A Catholic Perspective on the Purpose Driven Life,* contains an expanded version of the differences and clarifications together with agreement and enrichment comments delivered during those sessions.

At the same time, I offered suggestions for de-stressing one's life. They were based on *Slow Down,* a compilation of meditations designed to help achieve that purpose.

Over four years ago, I began broadcasting sixty-second inspirational spots over a local Clear Channel radio station. In preparation I met with their marketing and production people to discuss these proposed brief messages. They recommended a spiritual and religious, non-denominational and ecumenical approach, with the focus on what these persons judged to be the greatest challenge in today's world— coping with stress.

The spots thus became labeled as "Spiritual Suggestions to De-Stress Your Day." The repeated refrain at the end of each message was "You may have tried everything else, why not try God?"

Eventually Ave Maria Press saw in them the potential for a small devotional or inspirational book. *Slow Down* contains 100 of those spots with the addition of a spiritual suggestion and biblical phrase for each daily five-minute meditation. A collection of another 100 spots in similar, but slightly different format was recently released from Ave Maria Press in *Take Five: one hundred meditations to de-stress your days.*

As I mentioned, the suggestions at those sessions and described below grew out of *Slow Down*. With a nod to Stephen R. Covey and his very successful *The 7 Habits of Highly Effective People*, I have organized the material into "Seven Spiritual Suggestions to De-Stress Your Days."

Suggestion # 1
Be Still

The Columban Retreat and Conference Center at Derby, south of Buffalo and on the shore of Lake Erie, has a series of banners suspended by the side of the driveway leading to its main building. The words which greet visitors as they enter the compound combine into this phrase from a psalm: "Be still and know that I am God."

Retreatants arrive for an evening, a day, a weekend, or an entire week of quiet and reading, prayer and reflection.

Upon their departure, the reverse side of those banners sends them off with this blessing: "God be with you wherever you go."

The essential step for de-stressing one's busy life is to take a few minutes each day, perhaps only five minutes, to be still and rest in God.

Jesus did this; his faithful followers through centuries have done so; a contemporary medical study confirms the value of such reflection or meditation in reducing the symptoms of stress.

Luke's gospel demonstrates how Christ was a man of action and of prayer, a person who often healed, but regularly withdrew to pray in solitude.

For example, he cured a leper and also the great crowds who, having heard of this miracle, came and likewise asked for healing. But then the episode ends with this sentence, "He would withdraw to deserted places to pray" (Luke 5:12-16). In the very next chapter, curiously starting with the same numerical verse, Luke says, "He departed to the mountain to pray, and he spent the night in prayer to God." After this long period of praying, Jesus came down the mountain, selected the Twelve, continued his descent, and healed all who crowded around him (Luke 6:12-19).

To his twelve apostles, returning flushed with their own success at preaching and healing in his name, Jesus responded, "Come away by yourselves to a deserted place and rest awhile" (Mark 6:30-32).

St. Francis of Assisi frequently withdrew from his busy preaching and teaching efforts for a month in isolation to pray and reconnect with God.

Blessed Mother Teresa of Calcutta always required her Missionaries of Charity to begin and end a day of working with the poorest of the poor by spending an hour of meditative prayer in the morning and evening.

Popular author and lecturer on spirituality, the late Father Henri Nouwen, believed and taught that unless you have some time set aside each day for God and God alone, it will be impossible to transform your busy life into a constant awareness of the Divine Presence in your midst.

A medical study by Harvard cardiologist Dr. Herbert Benson indicated that people who had practiced some form of spiritual reflection once or twice a day experienced a remarkable reduction in the signs of stress (heart beat, blood pressure, sleep patterns).

Slow Down and *Take Five* provide some help in being still for a few minutes each day and experiencing how that simple step can help de-stress one's life. The following is the reading for Day 26 (*Take Five*, Ave Maria Press, p. 39):

Just Being

On the Amtrak train to Toronto, we passed high over a fairly substantial river or canal. Looking down from the coach windows, I saw several people sitting on a well-kept grassy area next to the water. They weren't really doing anything. They weren't eating around a picnic table, playing cards, or monitoring a group of children. They were just sitting there, presumably marveling at the beautiful day, enjoying the serenity that flowing water can give to our inner selves and appreciating one another's company.

In our society and culture, just being, just sitting and absorbing the beauty of life and relationships isn't easy.

There is the strong compulsion that we all seem to possess for pure action, to be doing something. But the Bible says: "Be still and know that I am God." That cluster of people sitting by the river's edge appeared—at least to my hopeful eyes—to be following that divine directive.

Spiritual Suggestion:

There are times when it is profitable just to *be* for a few moments and resist the need to *do* something that is outwardly productive.

Scriptural Thought:

"Mary kept all these things, reflecting on them in her heart."

Biblical Story:

The shepherds visit Mary and the child in Luke 2:15-20

Suggestion # 2
Exercise Regularly

Repeated studies emphasize that some regular exercise carries with it multiple benefits. We feel better, sleep more soundly, think more clearly; we can release tensions, regain our appetites, reduce our waistlines; we gain a doctor's approval, take satisfaction in the self-discipline required, enjoy the well-being produced by secreted endorphins.

In summary, we are healthier physically, mentally, and emotionally. Moreover, exercise also helps us spiritually because we seem to pray more effectively, conscious of the better care we are taking of the body God has given us.

In my pre-teen years I lived by a beautiful spring-fed body of water, one of the several Finger Lakes in New York State, and there developed a great love for swimming. As a college student at Notre Dame, I learned to play and enjoy the fascinating sport of handball. Over three decades ago, I was introduced to jogging, eventually running a marathon at Ottawa in my fifties.

After completing with a great deal of satisfaction the 26-mile marathon, I came to two conclusions: First, never to run another marathon! Second, getting an hour of exercise five days a week is a very desirable goal for me. I seldom perfectly fulfill that ideal, but am convinced of its value.

Often, when feeling mentally or emotionally fatigued, a long swim, fast handball game or a several mile run seems to rejuvenate me.

Those are all rather vigorous, endorphin-producing activities, even if I do them less intensely now at the age of 76. For many, perhaps the majority of people, their regular exercise may be somewhat less strenuous, like running on a treadmill or riding a stationary bicycle, walking in the mall or playing a round of golf, practicing yoga or swimming several dozen laps at a large pool.

While the type of activity is not really that critical, the truth of the matter remains that some type of exercise several times weekly on a consistent basis helps to reduce stress.

Suggestion # 3
Smile Often and Laugh Frequently

Larry Brennan and three other male nurses form a barbershop quartet and often give an hour-long presentation on

"Better Health Through Humor and Harmony." The four of them believe in this truth and back it up with medical data. Smiles and laughter, like the exercise we have just described, secrete endorphins and give us, if only temporarily, a sense of well-being.

Several times I have witnessed Larry and his quartet perform, twice before a support group of persons or families struggling with cancer. On every occasion the results were identical. People smiled and laughed and walked away feeling better, with spirits uplifted.

My experience with these nurses gave me a medical, theoretical and physical explanation of something I had sensed for decades. An audience, gathered for a classroom lecture, a large group presentation or a sermon/homily in church, react better and more positively when there is an occasional bit of humor in the remarks.

Similarly, I have found that a smile can lift myself or others out of a solemn, pensive mood. Even meeting a preoccupied stranger on the street, in an office building or at the mall and silently smiling at them can, sometimes, bring forth a smile in response.

We may have to push a bit to overcome our preoccupation and smile at another, but the very doing of this, even if there is not a positive reaction, brightens our own spirits.

Larry Brennan and his cohorts give this suggestion #3 about smiles and laughter a wellgrounded, scientific foundation.

Suggestion # 4
Practice Self-Giving

We cited in the earlier portion of this book the words of Pope John Paul II that the human heart is not content unless it is self-giving.

Just as forcing ourselves to smile when we seem preoccupied and feeling some tension can help us reduce stress, so, too, consciously practicing a small or significant act of self-giving can lift us out of that negative state.

Caroline Kennedy in her *A Patriot's Handbook* quotes a heroic story of self-giving from Senator John McCain about Mike Christian (pp. 16-17).

Christian grew up near Selma, Alabama, never had a pair of shoes until he was thirteen, but finished high school and, at seventeen, enlisted in the Navy. Mike became a pilot, was shot down over Vietnam, and spent a half-dozen years in a harsh prison.

While there he fashioned a crude American flag out of his prison blue shirt and two items sent to him from home—a white handkerchief and a red scarf. Every afternoon at 4:00 p.m., he and the other prisoners, including John McCain, fastened this flag to a wall and recited the Pledge of Allegiance.

Sometime later, guards discovered the flag, confiscated it, and as a lesson to all, badly beat him that night, finally throwing him back into the room with the other prisoners.

After comforting Christian the best they could, everyone went to sleep. McCain, in bed, but before dropping off looked over to a corner of the room, and there,under a naked light bulb, was Christian with another piece of white cloth and a piece of red cloth, his blue shirt and a bamboo needle. Despite eyes almost shut from the beating, he was making a second American flag, knowing how important this symbol was for himself and his imprisoned comrades.

Such stories of heroic self-giving cannot help but to inspire us to do likewise, even if on a lesser scale.

Suggestion #5
Smell the Roses

In Dan Brown's *Angels and Demons*, the Harvard symbologist Robert Langdon, more famous because of the novel and film, *The Da Vinci Code*, recalls as a young child hearing his mother begging her spouse "You need to take time to stop and smell the roses." Langdon's father apparently did not heed her advice and died a half-dozen years later of "cardiac" and "stress" (p. 53).

Thomas Moore, in his best-selling book, *Care of the Soul*, argues that beauty is arresting. It stops us in our tracks, removes us from everyday activities and leads us to transcendence. It can take us "out of the rush of practical life for the contemplation of timeless and eternal realities" (p. 278).

On a commuter plane from Albuquerque to Santa Fe, the pilot advised us that the short half-hour flight would feature particularly beautiful sights with the sunset and the colorful rocks or ridges. There were three passengers on the small aircraft. One never noticed the magnificent scenery (a failure to take the time to smell the roses); a second exclaimed,

"What a magnificent sight!"; the third prayed, "Praise God from whom all blessings flow."

The same reality. One never even saw it; the second did; the third went beyond the beauty to God, the creator of it all.

One fall day, I faced a thirty-minute drive out into the country. Some conflicts or challenges placed me in a heavy, preoccupied mood. However, the surrounding foliage was spectacularly beautiful and I could feel its pull on my troubled, stress-filled self. I finally let go, allowing the beauty and the Creator to impact me. The stress quickly dissipated.

To discover the beauty which leads us to God and peace one must first take time to smell the roses.

Suggestion # 6
See the Half-Full, Not the Half-Empty Glass

This suggestion deals not with the reality, but with our attitudes, how we perceive or regard the given situation—as a half-full or half-empty glass or challenge.

- The terrible terrorist event on 9/11 in New York City, the Pentagon and Pennsylvania exemplifies this principle.

  The incident viewed half-empty was the loss of life and the profound grief for so many as well as the traumatic shock to all Americans and others around the world over the emergence of global tension. This incident viewed half-full was the good which God brought out of such evil, the light in the midst of that bleak darkness. The enormous response of so many to help during and after that disaster was one positive interpretation of 9/11. The other, perhaps even more significant development, was the immediate reaction of most Americans to examine the priority that they were giving to their relationships. As soon as people learned of the terrorist attack, they almost instantly attempted to connect with those closest to them—spouses, children, parents, relatives and friends. And, at least for a period of time, Americans elevated relationships to a new level.

- Early on a Sunday morning, I opened up the church only to find a huge amount of debris—dirt and broken glass on and around the main altar. A large light fixture located in the ceiling 100 feet above the sanctuary had broken loose and crashed upon the marble below.

  I groaned over the mess, wondering how we could ever get this area cleaned-up and ready for the service in a half hour. We somehow did so. Later, as the celebrant in the middle of Mass, I thought to myself: "You idiot! If the light had fallen down during the liturgy, it could have killed or at least seriously injured you and others. The fact that this happened in the middle of the night was indeed a blessing.

- I was awakened around 3 a.m. in our parish house by the loud, shrill sound of a fire alarm. Almost immediately a telephone call from the security system headquarters informed me that the fire department was on its way. They arrived within minutes. I stood there in my pajamas as they swiftly and thoroughly checked our three-story, 90-year-old building for signs of fire. They found nothing. A faulty system had set off a false alarm. It was an embarrassing moment; an inconvenient interruption. But it could have been, instead, a disastrous fire. Half-empty, half-full.

- At 6:30 on a late fall, early winter morning, I walked outside to pick up the daily newspaper from the mail box. Starting down the three front steps, I was suddenly airborne and landed on my back with my left arm outstretched trying to break the fall.

My only fractured bones over seven decades of life had been my nose and some smashed fingers during those "minimal contact" handball games. But now I sensed uneasily and dreadfully that something had broken in my arm or wrist. Hours later the orthopedic hand specialist confirmed what was painfully evident: a major and bad break, a Colles fracture of my left wrist.

Since I am left handed, the injury created special problems and significant difficulties plus a cast for six weeks and two months of physical therapy. However, it could have been much worse—a broken leg, hip, or shoulder, or even a severe head injury.

Viewing these four instances as half-full or half-empty does not change the events, but alters our attitudes and helps the way we deal with them.

Suggestion # 7
Neither Worry Nor Fear

Pastor Rick Warren states that if God is the center of our lives, we worship; if not, we worry.

His words place Jesus' admonition about worry and fear in a modern context.

In the gospels, Christ speaks about dependence upon God (Matthew 7:25-34; Luke 12:21-31). The Lord tells us "Not to *worry* about your life"; "Can any of you by worrying add a single moment to your life-span?"; "Do not worry about tomorrow; tomorrow will take care of itself . . ."

Jesus backs up his exhortation by citing how God cares for the birds in the air and the flowers in the fields. If God does this for them, "Will he not much more provide for you, O you of little faith?"

The Lord's ultimate command and Warren's statement essentially coincide: "But seek first the Kingdom of God and his righteousness, and all these things will be given you besides."

God also tells us not to *fear*.

When Pope John Paul II stepped out upon the balcony of St. Peter's and delivered his initial message to the throng below him and to worldwide television viewers, the Holy Father's first words were; "Do not be afraid."

That phrase likewise began the gospel story of Jesus, reappeared during his preaching ministry, and concluded his teaching after the resurrection.

At the beginning, an angel of the Lord spoke identical words to Zechariah, Mary and the shepherds. "Do not be afraid . . ." (Luke 1:13; 1:30; 2:10).

Christ frequently reassured frightened followers during his public ministry. For example, when he came walking on the sea in the middle of the night, the disciples "were terrified" and "cried out in fear." Jesus immediately spoke to them, "Take courage, it is I. Do not be afraid" (Matthew 15:22-33).

Our fear and worry may focus upon the here and now or upon the life to come after death.

The biblical assurances we have cited above should calm our fears and worries about life on earth.

Jesus promises also that those who believe in him and who eat his body and drink his blood will live forever, will rise on the last day, will see God face to face in heaven. That prediction and pledge should similarly alleviate our fear and worries about the life to come after death.

About the Author

Father Joseph M. Champlin, former rector at the Cathedral of the Immaculate Conception in his home diocese of Syracuse, is now semi-retired and serves in sacramental ministry at Our Lady of Counsel in Warners, New York.

He has traveled over two million miles lecturing in the United States and abroad on pastoral subjects. Fr. Champlin has written more than fifty books. His works include *Together for Life* (Ave Maria Press) and *The Joy of Being an Altar Server* (Resurrection Press).

Basic Texts

Rick Warren, *The Purpose Driven Life* (Zondervan Corporation)

Joseph Champlin, *Slow Down* and *Take Five* (Ave Maria Press)

New American Bible (Catholic Book Publishing Corporation)

St. Joseph NEW AMERICAN BIBLES

FAMILY EDITION

Truly the most elegant of all. Here is an exceptionally fine Catholic Bible for the entire family to enjoy for many years. Durable sewn binding. Largest print of any Family Bible. Words of Christ printed in red. Over 100 Full-Color illustrations. Distinctive Family Record Section. GIFT BOXED. 1752 pages. 8½ x 11.

No. 612/97 ISBN 0-88842-612-3   **$55.95**

DELUXE GIFT EDITIONS
Full Size

Large, easy-to-read type, with 90 full-color illustrations, presentation page, colorful 8-page Family Record, Rosary & Stations in full color, over 70 photographs, Bible Dictionary, self-explaining maps, ribbon marker. Sewn binding. GIFT BOXED. 1696 pages. 6½ x 9¼.   **$44.50 each**

No. 611/13B Black Bonded Leather
ISBN 0-89942-971-8

No. 611/13W White Bonded Leather
ISBN 0-89942-972-6

No. 611/13BN Brown Bonded Leather
ISBN 0-89942-973-4

No. 611/13BG Burgundy Bonded Leather
ISBN 0-89942-970-X

DELUXE GIFT EDITIONS
Medium Size

Large, easy-to-read type, over 30 full-color illustrations, presentation page, colorful 8-page Family Record, Rosary & Stations in full color, Bible Dictionary, self-explaining maps, ribbon marker. Sewn binding. GIFT BOXED. 1632 pages. 5½ x 8⅛.   **$35.00 each**

No. 609/13BN Brown Bonded Leather ISBN 0-89942-959-9

No. 609/13W White Bonded Leather
ISBN 0-89942-958-0

No. 609/13R Red Bonded Leather
ISBN 0-89942-957-2

GIANT TYPE EDITIONS

magnificent edition of the New American Bible that features the largest type of any Catholic Bible in a comparable size. 6½ x 9¼. The focus is placed on the text, which is arranged for easy reading.   **$48.00 each**

No. 616/13BG Burgundy Bonded Leather ISBN 0-89942-584-4

No. 616/13GN Green Bonded Leather   ISBN 0-89942-622-0

STUDY EDITION

The most popular medium-size student edition available. Ideal for schools, CCD, and study groups. Special features include Large easy-to-read type, Bible Dictionary, self-explaining maps, Doctrinal Bible index, complete footnotes and cross-references, handy edge-marking index. 1632 pages. 5½ x 8⅛.

No. 609/04 ISBN 0-89942-950-5   **$8.95**

www.catholicbookpublishing.com

St. Joseph NEW AMERICAN BIBLES

PERSONAL SIZE EDITIONS

A convenient personal-size edition of the New American Bible. Contains many helpful aids for easy Bible reading and study. 32 full-color illustrations. 4-page presentation pages. 8-page Family Record section. Special features also include a Bible Dictionary, self-explaining maps, Dictrinal Bible index and complete footnotes and cross-references.Sewn bindings. 4½ x 6½. 1632 pages.

No. 510/10W White Imitation Leather
ISBN 0-89942-551-8   **$19.95**
No. 510/10BG Burgundy Imitation Leather
ISBN 0-89942-550-X   **$19.95**
No. 510/10BN Brown Imitation Leather
ISBN 0-89942-583-6   **$19.95**

No. 510/19BLU Blue Duotone Cover
ISBN 0-89942-534-8   **$26.95**
No. 510/19BN Brown Duotone Cover
ISBN 0-89942-533-X   **$26.95**

No. 510/23BG Burgundy Zipper Binding
ISBN 0-89942-576-3   **$29.95**
No. 510/23GN Green Zipper Binding
ISBN 0-89942-577-1   **$29.95**

No. 510/33BG Burgundy Magnet Binding
ISBN 0-89942-578-X   **$33.95**
No. 510/33GN Green Magnet Binding
ISBN 0-89942-579-8   **$33.95**

www.catholicbookpublishing.com

LITURGY OF THE HOURS
4-Volume Sets

This is the official English edition of the Divine Office that contains the translation approved by the International Committee on English in the Liturgy.

No. 409/10
Imitation Leather Binding
ISBN 0-89942-409-0
$145.00

Large Type Edition
No. 709/13
Color Leather Binding
ISBN 0-89942-710-3 **$195.00**

No. 409/13
Black Leather Binding
ISBN 0-89942-411-2
$169.00

No. 406/10
Flexible Maroon Cover
ISBN 0-89942-406-6 **$35.00**

CHRISTIAN PRAYER

Here are the official one-volume editions of the new internationally acclaimed *Liturgy of the Hours*. These new versions contain the complete texts of Morning and Evening Prayer for the entire year. The large-type edition is ideal for those with difficulty in reading. It has the same pagination as the regular edition.

Large Type Edition
No. 407/10
Flexible Maroon Cover
ISBN 0-89942-407-4 **$37.00**

Large Type Edition
No. 418/10
Flexible Maroon Cover
ISBN 0-89942-453-8 **$17.95**

SHORTER CHRISTIAN PRAYER

Contains Morning and Evening Prayer from the Four Week Psalter and selected texts for the Seasons and Major Feasts of the year. It is ideal for Parish use.

No. 408/10
Flexible Maroon Cover
ISBN 0-89942-408-2
$13.95

www.catholicbookpublishing.com